In Love... &War

The Anthology of Poet Warriors

Vol. I

-DEDICATION-

To the doctors and staff at Marcus Institute for Brain Health, and all of the other health care professionals working tirelessly to help our nation's veterans overcome the wounds of war.

-CONTRIBUTING POETS-

-INTRODUCTION-

To my knowledge, this collection is somewhat of a first.

The book in your hand was written by more than three dozen contributors of varied background and experience. Some of the contributors are award-winning poets, others are best-selling authors. Some have advanced degrees in the craft of writing. Some have never before been published. In fact, many poets included in this collection have never even shared a piece of their writing publicly before now.

The one thing they all have in common is service to their nation. You see, every poem you are about to read was written by a veteran to help bring you a better understanding of the experience of war—directly from those who've tasted it, smelled it, felt it, and been branded by it. Each war experience falls along an endless spectrum. No two tales or interpretations will ever be identical. This collection of warrior poetry is as raw and unbridled as war itself.

Far too much of the current public opinion about the reality of war, and military service in general, is derived from actors, directors, producers, and writers who never spent a day in uniform. An unfortunate fact considering there are countless brilliant, hard-working, unemployed veteran creatives in each of those respective fields. I digress.

This project serves to provide a platform for talented veteran writers to showcase their ability and deliver priceless insight to the reality of military life, as well as war. Thereby helping bridge the gap between veteran and civilian. The outcome is a product which serves the veteran community. One hundred percent of the profits from the sales of the book in your hand go to GallantFew, a veteran-run charity whose mission is to facilitate a peaceful, successful transition from military service to a civilian life filled with hope and purpose. So thank you. You've already helped support a veteran in need simply by purchasing this book.

No writing prompts were given to the contributors of this book; simply submit poetry and a short bio. That created the immense challenge of organizing 38 completely different writing styles, without a congruent central theme, into a single anthology.

Despite the vast array of contributors, each possessing a distinct viewpoint on the subject of war, certain recurring concepts emerged throughout this collection. Themes of physical and mental preparation, forging of unbreakable bonds, humor, horror, and the lasting ramifications of what it means to have served one's country all consistently permeate the ink on these pages.

Our best efforts have been applied to divide the entries into four categories that most intuitively encompass those concepts, in an attempt to give a loose timeline of the military experience.

The anthology opens with Preludes & Prologues, a section primarily dealing with how one's youth shaped their decision to join the military, as well as military training itself.

In Love... explores the forging, and in some cases destruction of, valued relationships as a result of military service.

&War, without question, is the meat of this book. The vivid, searing descriptions provided in this section of the war a soldier lives in combat are rivaled only by the heartbreaking tales of the ensuing war fought internally, which inevitably follows us home.

We finish with Epilogues & Epitaphs. The poetry in this section pulls no punches and provides no quarter. Candid memorials commemorate the immortal bonds of brotherhood, written alongside poignant reflections and introspections of self, war, the world, and our place in it.

WITH WEIGHT OF WARS, THESE WORDS WE WIELD
To pierce fierce, once more, spurious mail and shield.
Exposed to mute the typecast, bloodlust brute
Naked. Unafraid.
Behold this scarred but healing heart,
beating warrior's ink.

- Leo Jenkins

-PRELUDES & PROLOGUES-

You and Me

Tricycles painted red in blood,
Campfire's charcoal—camouflaged faces black,
Lighter fluid melts toys in the mud,
And we're off to Hell and back.

You and me,
Up the tree,
Or recreating Valley Forge.
Juggle the snakes,
Juggle their venom,
Then skateboard Springfield Gorge.

Hair would sprout,
And licenses divulge;
Car tires the screaming beast.
We'd trade wizards for women,
Vow to die hurt, young, and poor,
But wild hearts would stay wild at the least.

You and me,
Destined to be,
Blood-spillers of legend and lore.
At eight steep thrills,
At eighteen cheap pills,
And at nineteen I joined the Corps.

-David Rose

Bones

Stood in the garage beneath a dying light.
My old man looked out at the sky with a look of fright.
He finished his cigarette and beer with a sigh.
I didn't speak up, not a word from the mouth.
Just as he expected, now looking south.
"Always a quiet one," he said through cigarette breath.
He nodded at nothing, and lit up again.
As I left, not knowing when I'd see him again.
Gave him a hug, in a drought of dread.
He looked me in the eye, and bid me farewell.
Told me I'd soon embark upon the seas he knew so well.

-Ryan Kisner

Full Of Tradition

As I hold my A2 with minimal practice,
The drill instructor screams, "You fucking maggots!!"
Go-fasters and glow belts just out of receiving, Straight up boots, naïve and willing.
We move faster and faster, being pushed to our limits.
Then we pushed past that with a sharp left pivot. Initial drill and field day all for fun,
Heading into the woods, following compass under moon and sun.
The United States Marine Corps is full of tradition From 1775 to post-9/11.

-Justin Eggen

Boom, Bap, Crack and Pop

I was 5, maybe
When I found what destroyed others and saved me
Dad dragged home a barrel of toy guns and I loved it
Swords, pop guns and muskets.

I was 9, maybe
When I learned about Brenda's baby why we're crazy
Mom brought home a box of rap cassettes, I ate it up
Raekwon tape played so much my box ate its guts

Neither took the other's hints
Neither liked the other's gifts
Neither took the other's shit
Neither liked the other

I learned a lot back then about conflict and kids
Playing war, listening to songs about kills
Staying in that house, hearing fights through walls about kids
About parents and leaders pushing conflict on innocent kids

I learned a lot since then but I hold on to it still
Pounding pavement, perusing prose about life's thrills
Stashing mentors and leaders, where wisdom exists
Passing on action, learning in vacuums to live

-Keith Dow

Dress for Success

Before a man in uniform
I was the man of the house
I was 8 years old when my father moved out
Before a man in uniform
I had felt self-doubt
Lost identity with nothing figured out

Before a man in uniform
I was a kid that was ignorant
Youthfully clueless and aware of evil's existence
Before a man in uniform
I was shy to diligence
My future plans were scarce and never consistent

Before a man in uniform
You would never believe this
One bold choice and that was to enlist
Before a man in uniform
You wouldn't thank me for my service
Respect the man and then the uniform
Because a man has more than one purpose

-Tyler James Carroll

Bittersweet

This one time, it was all about mysterious places and cammied faces
An unspoken English dialect, like mumbled screams and big eyeballs
with throbbing jugulars
A musical rhythm with every step and acute peripheral vision
Methodical and ritualistic
Absurd yet automatic, but normal and endured
Irony and comic relief are an unsatisfactory justification for the reality of
things
Addicted to the possibility of things
Obsessing about the policy of things
But then there were nights that were quiet and cold
With the muffled static of roger, check, roger…
And skies that couldn't have been painted by hand
Only ambushed by epiphany
At peace with the worst because that's protocol
Things that cannot be unlearned, but unleashed
Empty eyes, dirty skin
Swollen mind, dirty sin
Expunged in the name of Good Will
Ahhhhh, but bittersweet, indeed.

-Nick Misiano

Endless Pursuit

Towering, serrated, white-capped rock mimics beauty
Some nights are longer than others, not because I sense monotony
It's just that time of year; we thrive in the blackness of night
A low moon and veiling clouds bid us providence

Walking like ants in a column and with the same sense of purpose
Filthy creek water, sticky air, it never rains here
Dirt, gravel, and grease muddy up my hair from under my carapace
I chew on leaves, spitting black, it settles me in this discomfort

We'll find you, we always do
We'll ascend mountains, we'll ford rivers and
Leave behind nothing except that still tranquility
I used to know, before I came here.

-Clay Hildreth

Illustrator: Justin Craine

Stay Wild

As a child I'd collect devils claws, roam the desert naked with coyotes,
javelinas and hawks.
Days filled with my palo verde tree fort, sun and monsoons
dissolved into objectives grades boys the night and moon.

Como La llorona canta los almas del ontoño
Señor oscuro nos bendiga con los verdades duro

Fear the thief sabotaged the alarms invaded inner
Peace rests in your Heart. Not in distant places or in people's arms
But it's a lonely trek and the life is
Overly disciplined underly sexed
It is only after the deepest darkness that the greatest light will come.
Like
-Malcolm X

Hard work corrodes the chains and scars ask "Who are you, Mia?"
This is perfect, that is perfect, from the perfect, springs the perfect. If the
perfect is taken from the perfect, the perfect remains. Like
-Sri Guru Gita

Stay wild
Divination initiation illumination
Demands your participation
Horned Teachers are hunting you bloody spears drawn and drooling in
anticipation
Fears become your school
And their corpses your tools
Their death cries are those of the universal soul rules

Gravity over vanity
Orbiters over followers
Waking life orgies over pornologers
Third ays over Instagram likes
Shadow wisdom over love and light
Hype
Don't believe
Truth is
Stellar nurseries over obituaries and Gregorian time pieces
Unity over conspiracy
And what's on TV

Now the devils claws collect the child
The coyote begins to smile
With cactus hanging from the heart
As the desert myths and allegories
Stay wild

-Mia Quintanilla

School Circle

Sit kneel bend if you drink don't drive if you drive don't drink don't marry a stripper wrap it before you tap it check her ID twice seventeen will get you twenty if you get arrested go ahead kill yourself because I'll kill then skull fuck you on Monday morning for doing stupid shit update your will update your page two and the RED make sure your mom or dad or wife or kid gets your life insurance if you get killed pack light freeze at night junk on the bunk hydrate hydrate hydrate go to dental go to medical sweat more in peace bleed less in war run fast run far shoot straight kill first be at the armory at zero five draw weapons form up forward march fire superiority is the best medicine so keep shooting don't stop push forward keep shooting call a Corpsman but don't stop keep shooting keep moving stack up kick in the door frag out clear your corner clear the room stack up clear your corner clear the room black bag zip tie turn him over head count ammo count chow's continuous stand post jack shack form up forward march turn in weapons sight count up say goodbye dog tags Kevlar boots rifle hand salute Taps dismiss.

-Michael Ramos

-Preludes & Prologues-

One Man

Several hands raised after standing afoot
"Send me!" If not, then who?
Call it free will or cojones
Less than one percent of ninety-nine jabronis
Rushing through time to stand in line
Poked and prodded; sever the carotid
Shaved heads and ridicule; minuscule
Broken down and built back up
Raw character refined
Hurry up and wait
Be first through the door
Don't hesitate
On the other side with his AK
Spray and pray to such dismay
Roaming this purgatory, Infidel wins the day
Back on the block, the swag is a bit straighter.
Bellowing from the bowels, "laugh now, cry later!"
My home is a bomb crater
I'm a mother-fuckin' soul agitator
Left foot planted firm; backbone stern
Out yonder lies the horizon
Over the next berm

-Nick Misiano

Lost Boys

We are the Lost Boys.
The forgotten boys,
Who came from broken homes.
Our fathers walked out early,
Our mamas blamed us since the womb.

We are the Lost Boys.
Garrison's not for us boys.
Our hair's out of regs and sometimes we might,
Show up to PT hungover,
From drinking, and fucking, and getting in fights,
And living the free life of a rover.

We are the Lost Boys.
The never gonna grow up boys,
Bangarang is what we yell,
When Route Hyena turns
into the highway to hell.

We are the Lost Boys.
You can always count on us boys.
Because when the going gets tough,
Toy soldiers get scuffed,
But it ain't shit for those that live rough.

-Joe Barnhill

Illustrator: Justin Craine

Jargon

Reveille, reveille,
Hard charger,
Motivate,
High and tight,
Full up round,
Good to go,
Hurry up and wait,
What's your Pos?
Foot patrol,
Inbound,
4 MAMs,
RPG,
Contact right,
Weapons free,
Corpsman up!
Medevac,
Dress Blues,
Taps, taps,
lights out.

-Michael Ramos

The Birds

The most beautiful birds
burn in your ears
before taking off into
jet black night.
Don't mourn.
They might return
tailhook caught up in your
arresting gear.
Aren't we all just clinging to wire?
Until tomorrow—
New Mission
cat shot into
darknessfasterthansound.
The most beautiful birds
fly to kill.

-Laura Hamlet

Sacred Profanity

The unhallowed masses gather
in the pre-dawn darkness
cursing the First Sergeant's decree
that the weather warranted short-sleeved PTs

Expostulations make puffs of condensation
above the huddled heads

Curses: decrying the hierarchy
the weather, the looming duty day

Expostulations and expectorations
phlegm rattling like drum rolls in barrel chests
snot rockets projected from nasal passageways
the asphalt anointed with fluid
spattered with the inevitable effluvia
from the several dozen dippers
their mouths and lips lugubriously distended
with massive wads of tobacco

Meanwhile, in the aid station, the medic
Christ-like, extends lifelines of saline solution
to the several hangover cases
who were awake just three hours ago
playing beer pong in the barracks

The medic imparts no judgment
only the life-giving sacrament
salvation in a plastic bag
that flows directly into their veins

Granted their reprieve
the prodigals hurry to rejoin the congregation
which is shuffling into a semblance of a formation

The Company Commander
flanked by the First Sergeant arrive
pastor and penance collector
attention, roll call
A terse, lifeless sermon from the CO
concluding with the blessing and dismissal
"Squad leaders take charge, conduct PT"

The rite concluded, the congregation fragments
and the real worship begins

The stocky squad leaders taking their squads
to the subterranean temple to pray at the iron altar
the lithe squad leaders bound into the twilight like antelope
their subordinates sprinting to keep up

The uttered oaths replaced with the deeper, silent ones

Litter carries around the airfield
Hill sprints, hauling teammates, water jugs
obstacle courses, rope climbs

In the darkness, the trite rites, gripes, curses
are replaced by primal grunts and groans
gasps for air

The inarticulate fragments of sound
as the truly sacred can only be given such broken notes

For words would only cheapen
the unspoken oaths silently affirmed
there in the pre-dawn dark

-Jonathan Baxter

Scribbled in Blood on a State Department Wall

I worked with guys who joined 'cuz it was their religious duty.
I worked with guys who were answering a call.
They worked with guys who were upholding a family tradition.
They worked with thugs,
Who worked with pretty boys,
Who borrowed CLP from rednecks,
Who swapped porno mags with rich kids.
Conservatives. Libs. Ex-stoners. Atheists and Christians of every damn
denomination.
Men who joined who loved competition,
Competing for range-high with men who wanted to get out of some
boring-ass town,
Sharing a barracks room with those out to earn the respect of a dad,
To make a girl sorry,
...or to touch a dragon's tail.

Every walk of American life—
Except those out to liberate an Iraqi,
Or to trade in the ancient skill of killing for much anything else.

-David Rose

Civilization and Strife

A dog bounced, yipping and yapping, clamoring for affections.
Fat of belly, soggy of flesh, and tender of feet,
though he was no longer a "he;" in gender a defeat.
Evolved and progressed, soft and voluminous,
he/it loudly consumed at "Vocif 'R Us,"
and lonely, clawlessly, shat out his slumberous soul.
"Civilization" was his name, a fevered pitch of ease.

The wild gave way to his slobbering bark, blown away
by his haughty enlightenment, reason and strength unheeded.
His claws were vestigial, his teeth removed, unneeded.
An endless maelstrom of directions, a wide road was his domain,
leading nowhere and nohow, widening into a plain.
Yet alone, he consumed in a storm of cowardice,
and courage was a curse to him.

Away from this fat spectre loped a pack.
Ancient and terrible, lean and functional, they ran,
in flares of grey, black, brown, and tan.
They too consumed, but garbage and leavings they did not scour.
They hunted, they tore, they shattered, and devoured.
As many, they ran as one, complete in function and form;
Effectual, advantageous, a study in terrible utility.

No worthless part was on their streamlined bodies,
 "Pretty" and "Soft" were their curses, "Beauty" as worthless a pledge.
A narrow path, a ray in math, thinned before them to a cutter's edge,
 "Red in Tooth and Claw" they were, stripped of voluptuous fat,
worshipping their gods with blood, gore, and violent habitat.
Their name was "Strife." Their name was "Power."
The fathers of all that makes men great.

-Cokie

-IN LOVE-

Never Forget

In love, we fell,
like two towers;
burning, crumbling.
Like silence of solitude shattered.

In love, we rose,
like a nation;
unity born of agony.
Like the old gift of living, resurrected.

In love, we see, blessed,
like the blind;
no color, no politics.
Like unconditional Never Forgets.

We made love,
like a slogan
carved it on the everywhere
like fear. Like time doesn't own us all.

We remembered love
like burning, crumbling, & agony.
the other parts went dormant
like living, resurrection, & unity...

Until the next time we fall.

-Leo Jenkins

Reconciling With My First Love

(Originally published in Havok Journal)

Fresh and new,
Waiting on the shelf.
The Beret, hunter green,
pillowy with felt.
The Flash
Yellow, red, white, and blue
Sits atop the table.
Rank beside, everything askew.
Dull and smudged,
the Jump Boots remain.
The event is tomorrow,
time wanes away.
Needle and thread,
golden yellow, a border match.
Do these hands remain?
Turn by turn, catch by catch
Midnight thirty
the sewing done.
Thumbs pricked, blood drawn,
Beret and Flash are One.
Rag and brush
glowing heels and toes
One A.M.
Ready to wear. Soon, time to go.
Sleep and morning
Boots laced and tied
Dark blue jacket, ribbons
and badges, side by side.
Green Beret.
There she patiently sits
Flash sewn on, rank affixed
shaved and formed. Ready.
18 months,
together again
Green Beret donned.
First loves, reconciled.

-Marshall McGurk

-In Love-

Hands Holding You Close

Lying there, in a world of bliss; heart pounding, deep breaths, inhale, exhale..... Arms wrapped around your waist, whispers of deep affections tickle your ear. Pulled in closer, heart to your back, beating, thump, thump, thump, You see headlights in the window and a few seconds later the front door open and you never realized I'd be home this early. Two hearts race together, beating faster and harder. THUMP, THUMP, THUMP! Your mind racing on excuses that I'll never believe. "I was lonely and he was there for Me.", "I didn't mean to, I swear.", "I was going to tell you." Stairs creaking as I slowly sneak up to the bedroom, not to wake you. I open the door, you go to scream, "Stop!" but it's too late, I drop the flowers and throw the ring in your direction. Front door SLAMS! And headlights pull off in the distance. A hand on your shoulder, as the tears stream down your face and hit the floor. You lay with him and let his arms wrap around you once again. You whisper. "I hate you." Not knowing if you're talking to him or yourself. Close your eyes and let your mind fade, as you realize he's never coming back and you just couldn't wait one more night alone.

-Michael Krukowski

My Whore, My Corps

I've always lusted for my whore
Although I can lay claim to her, she is not mine and she doesn't need me
After our years together, she grew on me like an epiphyte
But to her, I was just another wanderer; just another number in the night
I was born from her womb; a bastard with lava rocks in my pocket
With a sun-beaten neck tan, I learned her savage ways
Her holidays and history was my ego-ridden playground
With my prowess, I discovered every inch of her, but still left with mysteries abounding
Ohhhhhh! I loved her so
Soooo unattainably so
She is my lustful memory
Sold to young men, exposing their manhood for posterity
But they never own her soul by ripping through her hole
She belongs to her gods, her legends, and her rageful ghosts
She popped my cherry, graduating my brain from a good washing
I hope she stays ruggedly, beautiful with lyrical contempt
I hope she remembers my friends
Alas…before you get stuck inside of her; pink mist
Leave her behind
She is smothering
She is busy and spitefully blind
Our affliction is one of love and hate
You love her, but she hates you
You don't fuck her, she fucks you
She taxes that ass and rakes your soul
She doesn't need your resentment
She has plenty of other hard dicks to fuck and ride the pole
But you cherish her for all those amazing times together
She taught you cool tricks and things
She's that unicorn of a score that keeps you coming back for more
Yearning…long after it's over and our time is up
Oh! It's definitely been over between us for some time now
I'm still lingering for another round
Because I still dream about our nights in the jungle
Or when we frolicked over volcanic wastelands
Or wasted away on mounds of concrete rubble
My whore is the valley, deep inside of her trough
Darkness is where the heart lives
She was my lust and my love
My whore, my Corps
Nowadays, she doesn't know me anymore, but I know her still
And some things will remain as they will

-Nick Misiano

-In Love-

Responsibility

Father & son - Shooter & gun
Who's held responsible?
Hand & hand they walk - Hand & handle they talk
When did truth become pliable?
If lies deceit - I want retreat
to something reliable

Subject to subjectivity - Value is in creativity
Words crash into a roadblock
Pen & paper - Responsibility of a creator
When will the judgment stop?
Better sooner than later - Bitter is the flavor
Of a face without a clock

-Tyler James Carroll

My Beautiful Helmand

Ohh my beautiful Helmand
With your streams lined with trees
It's difficult to picture them
Without the snapping leaves

Oh my beautiful Helmand
With your fields that always flood
I wish I could remember their smell
Without seeing a pool of blood

Oh my beautiful Helmand
I'll always hold you dear
You left me with beautiful memories
And a ringing in my ears.

-Jonathan O'Brien

-In Love-

Scars

She was the bravest woman I have ever met lying there with me in the dark of night, feeling all the scars on my heart and yet standing her ground.

-Nicholas Rossin

My Rifle

When I got your number, I memorized it instantly, forever looking
forward to that first trigger pull. Everything about you I was attracted
to—
The R.O.F., iron sights, and the way you felt in my hands. At first touch I
fell in love with the cold alloy. Learning you inside and out, I was
overjoyed. Knowing I'll never forget all that I've learned.
Even after so many trigger pulls, you always performed.

-Justin Eggen

Untitled (Be Strong, My Son)

Be strong, my son. Be strong.
Let your arms not forsake work,
let your back not forget weight.
Make your muscles hard and hungry,
your spine unyielding and straight.
Let hardness be your trait!
Be strong, my son. Be strong,
for I am your father,
and the Lord is your God!

Be brave, my boy. Be brave.
Leave the ways of the coward,
be the one called "Bold!"
In desperate times, be the measure,
though times are bleak and cold.
Be courageous to behold!
Be brave, my son. Be brave,
for I am your daddy,
and the Lord is your God!

Be honorable, my lad. Be honorable.
Abide by the code of your tribe,
from your men earn only respect!
Show your worth to your brothers,
let threats fear your group, and redirect.
Their values you should perfectly reflect!
Be honorable, my lad. Be honorable,
for I am your father,
and the Lord is your God!

Be skillful, my bairn. Be skillful.
Let your handiwork have merit,
lend worth to your trade.
Let your calloused hands use tools,
a hammer, nails, a blade.
Let them marvel at what you have made!
Be skillful, my bairn. Be skillful,
for I am your father,
and the Lord is your God!

Be dangerous, my child. Be dangerous.
No man is good who is also weak,
nor does merit come from the willfully frail.
Let your arms be a mighty wind,
your mind a fearless gale.
Let strife make you prevail!
Be dangerous, my child. Be dangerous,
for I am your father,
and the Lord is your God!

Be loving, little man. Be loving.
Let your wife know your heart,
your children your tender embrace.
Show devotion to your family,
let them see God's grace.
Your fondness should be commonplace!
Be loving, little man. Be loving,
for I am your father,
and the Lord is your God!

Be honest, my heir. Be honest.
Say what you will do.
Do what you will say.
Tell the truth despite the consequences,
as long as it is called "Today."
Do it daily, come whatever may!
Be honest, my heir. Be honest,
for I am your father,
and the Lord is your God!

Be holy, young one. Be holy.
Study the Scriptures,
and learn the ways of God.
Control your passions and desires,
and choose the right path to trod.
Be more than just a righteous façade!
Be holy, young one. Be holy,
for I am your father,
and the Lord is your God!

-In Love-

Be wise, little friend, be wise.
Read the books and learn the facts,
the history, the math, the science.
Do not be dull and stupid,
or on simple thoughts place your reliance!
Against foolishness scream your defiance!
Be wise, little friend. Be wise,
for I am your father,
and the Lord is your God!

Be better, my son. Be better.
Many sins have I committed,
many mistakes have I made.
Learn from my many faults.
avoid the prices I have paid.
Do not be afraid to
Be better, my son. Be better
even more than your father,
for the Lord is your God!

-Cokie

A Family Tradition

Me or the bottle,
And he chose the bottle over me.
Now it's war or you, Baby,
Just the way it's gotta be.

-David Rose

A Great Plain Love Song

For the first time today
All the sweetest savories I thought but never had,
All the holiest hallelujah my throat dashed
Against barewall afters
to echo empty space TV rays,
Rush in my olfactory.
Dervish across my buds.

All the sweetest savories curl,
sens-smoking finger wrap
                         around
          my mind
...and...
I
Am
bline

Sun dazzled on a crystal beach,
fumble lost in the viscera Mark Twain made America's words of.
I never have uttered a 'hallelujah'.
I never have been a thunderhead.
Silent. Light arcing.
pinkslateblack on the horizon.

I crackle lightning.
I am air pressure-suspended rain,
Autumn's precious wrecking force.

Winterdream approaching prairie
Flies me with her breath,
Like a cat bats a feather.

-Paul Martinez

By the Faith of Man

a sonnet on camaraderie in the military

It's creating something out of nothing
It's sharing toothpaste and toilet paper
It's knowing how to tell when they're bluffing
It's clinging tightly to hope's vapor
It's swapping stories and photos of kids
It's telling tales of woe into the night
It's wiping tears from your wingman's eyelids
It's keeping vigil until dawn's first light
It's mandatory fun and laughing loud
It's raising glasses to those brutal years
It's sheltering you from the maddening crowd
It's endless days of toil, blood, sweat, and tears
It's never having to face it alone
It's folding flags at silent, gray headstones

-Robin Ludwig

-In Love-

I, started the words that ended, U.

there was adoration in her eyes. a spark like silence dancing naked in front of a mirror. her tongue tasting the way it should, like honey, like lies, like a swarm of bees after the honey. those soft fingers untangling the hard knot that constricted us, those hard hands constricting the soft parts of us. it went on like this for hours, for seven lifetimes.
the colors rose and fell and became aware of the moonlight dancing on shadows from the future.
she breathed into us one last time, shed a hard tear from her eye to mine and we collapsed within each other at the dying light of dawn when the drugs fell off and all we were left with was ourselves, entwined in the memory of tomorrow, blinded by forever.

-Leo Jenkins

Of Mars

Us—we are of Mars;
Cold.
Male.
Together while alone,
As alone while together, sure.
Those not from Mars;
Revile and condemn,
And putrefy of us that which is pure.

-David Rose

Third Wheel

Obey the web of lies
spun by the internet.
Antidote from the poison
a relationship with commitment.
A crowd pleaser,
love is between two people, isn't it?
A fallacy – intimacy
is no longer intimate.

-Tyler James Carroll

Metaphors

Oh, false world, fill your pages with comparisons,
Your thin papers with metaphors!
Let my life be real, a thick and tangible thing,
Drinking of the rich blood of actuality!

More than "like" or "as,"
More than airy ink on featureless paper.
Let the ink be puckered scars and experience,
my soul and flesh the searing pages.

Banish from me the easy lies,
smoke and similes sweet to the mind.
Those mere mirrors of lost chance
pouring through limp, untested fingers.

Give me more than coffeehouse prose,
that decaf Chicken Soup for the Gutless.
Throw me to the wolves and beasts!
Let me fight, bite, test my might!

Let shallow movies not define my Love,
those platforms of simple fuckery.
Let me find naked flesh and mortal bone,
And skin electric worth memorizing.

Let me create a roaring life with my Love,
With a kiss, a moan, and a sigh
To contrast against the pale, bleak, and
disguised meaninglessness.

Let that Life bound outward
Giggling, growing, leaping
with the control of a sprinting bonfire
On a dry September day!

-In Love-

Give me Battle and wild War,
For the sake of the barbaric fight!
Politics and vomitus reasons be damned,
Like the yellow First World contests and bouts.

Let me feel the voluptuous red, hear the blood,
Roaring through arteries stretched to snapping,
leaving behind delights and woes
Too light, relaxed, and sweet for a warrior's stomach.

-Cokie

Or am I Human

Insecure...

Everyone sees me stand tall, but inside you wouldn't believe how small I really feel...

They see a smile and soulful laugh, but I hear the cries of a soul that feels alone.
You can see me, but do you really see me?
Do you see how my life isn't easy?
How my friends confide in me, how I give every breath to everyone around me?
Some who ask how I am, aren't the ones who should really care...
Family just expects me to get through, little do they know I am barely holding on...
It's a tightrope balancing act with a smile on my face...
You only see one side of this eclipse because darkness isn't a pretty face.

I hold myself up, because my bones are strong, but my spirit isn't what my body portrays.
I can use a compliment... or two, but is it
an insecurity to reach for love, to beg for affirmation?

But damn, don't you think I deserve that once in a while? Don't you think I earned it?

I act selfless, but I am always looking over my shoulder for some sign of appreciation.

I can't help it, this is me. Am I needy, or am I human? Am I broken and just need the right touch? Or am I just tired of doing too much?
I feel like I have so much depth, I have so many sides, and maybe that's why I never feel fulfilled.
Deep you say?
Well, I wish I was shallow... not in the sense you are thinking, but in the sense of being easy to fill.

I don't get why I am needing love, needing a touch or maybe a hug. It's something I need, to be able to hold onto at a time I feel like I am falling...

-In Love-

One finger after another keeps losing grip, I can only hold on for so long.

Shake this feeling, you are better than this,
pick your head up and smile because everyone expects it.

Smile and wave, smile and wave

Look at my perfect life on Facebook, look how happy I am.

Keep smiling kid you have them all fooled

Stand up tall and walk proud.
I carry the weight of one man and it's more than the world will
understand.
How long can I keep up this pace? When will I be done with this race?

All I want to be is a good man....

I make mistakes, but do the best I can with just a promise to keep waking
up, trying, to be a good man.

A voice in my head- "The world is counting on you...."

-Vincent Vargas

Relationship with Music

The keys of a piano
    unlocked a door that revealed
      my emotions.
The strings of a guitar
    wove a pattern that structured
      commotion.
The beat of a drum
    pulsed life back into
      a body's heart.
The melody of her voice
    measured our tenor
      from the start.

-Tyler James Carroll

With Her, I'm Walking

Exposed toes on jagged roads
made of pebbles, pebbles made of stones,
stones made of boulders, boulders made from, who knows?
Ambition, a stones' throw, a road grown, home.
Each breath extending, a finite stride, yet never-ending.
Pass along our final steps, ascending. Pass on everything.
Pass on the pebbles made of stones. Pass on the boulders made from,
who knows.
Pass on the clothes, pass on the shoes that mute these jagged roads.
Step on the feet; the defeat of thorns, the wild ones adorn with dirty knees.
Step on believing we survive these things. Step on the wars that make us men.
Step on the sights we'll never see again. Step on the day. Step on the night.
Step on believing, despite the familiar jagged road is nowhere in sight.

-Leo Jenkins

Our New Firefight

You're a different kind of enemy, fire
Yea, you're a natural part of things
But not when you're running nuclear
That's where we come in, comrades all
And we'll stand to our lines, you hungry bitch
Dirt and smoke, planes in the sky
Mech and infantry, in your way we stand
Being small in something big again
Yea, I'm home.

-Jim Bartlett

Gin and Limes

I used to fear clear liquor
Too many bad times I can't remember
A neighbor's porch destroyed
An ex-girlfriend annoyed
A fight with my jaw obliterated
But those were many moons ago,
Clear liquor is now my cure
and there is nothing left to fear.

-Dwight Buchanan

Warlord

I have fought many wars.
But none have been so just
as protecting your heart my queen!

-Nicholas Rossin

-In Love-

My Struggle is like a War

They simper over iPhones and running water,
While I am gifted bone, blood, bayonet, and bullets
To Fight, and Fight against, in the foreign dirt.

Let my God be found real and full,
Untamed, worthy of fierce worship!
Let the weak deities fade and die,
Blown by the vitreous smoke of His passing!

Give me surety of His strength, might,
and judgement, tempered with mercy
A God worth trembling before
Rather than guessing at.

Let me find Brotherhood!
Let me be needed in the fevered mud,
So my arms will not be empty, idle.
I carry and am likewise carried.

Let my Brothers be an unrivaled rivalry,
No mere boys' club.
We chant the songs of strength!
We Fight the songs of youth!

Prodigals, killers, dilated braggarts,
They mean more than placid acquaintances.
Emptied of Self, my Brothers selflessly bear
My weight and soul, and I Theirs.

Some men by metaphors do not live,
Or scrape about with cheap imitations.
They find Strength for their Strife,
And seek Strife for the Strength.

Their life is distilled in pure vitality
Who love their Women, bring forth
a Child, seek a Fight, serve their God,
and adopt Brothers with blood-soaked arms.

-Cokie

I Struggle with Being Alone

I always want it, but I don't always like it,
I always need it, but my heart feels defeated,
Because the walls don't talk, and neither does Samson.
Maybe a king's ransom, will handsomely
Reward me, with someone or something,
But I'm far from a king,
Though heavy is my crown,
Of heartache and frowns,
And it slowly brings me down…here.
Looking into this mirror,
I see the absence of sleep in your eyes, again,
Standing amidst the silence of men,
At war.
I've seen this place before,
This sink, this drain, this floor.
Shuffling through the haze,
When did I lose track of the days,
And when did I last eat,
And how long have I been on my feet?
The, pressure is building,
And I'm feeling concerned,
Because these four fingers burn,
When my elbows turn, a certain way.
And suddenly, I remember that day.
The blunt force of the explosion,
Caused what feels like corrosion
In these nerves, as they tingle,
And every single, time they do
I'm reminded of you, and your sand.
And that, is the whole truth pure and simple.
But, the truth is rarely pure and never simple.

-Emilio Gallegos

-In Love-

Love Letters to Death

I've been writing love letters to death
I've been sending signals to the dead
Wishing I could erase the dysfunction from my brain
Hoping I can escape the darkness I've created
I've been writing love letters to death
But she doesn't seem to want to reply
I beckon for her to come close
But she stays just out of reach
Siren songs of half dead impulse lure my heart to despair
I've been writing letters to death
On wings of fallen angels
Waiting to see them fly once again
Broken wings defying aerodynamics creating lift
Out of the darkness
Out of the depths
I've been writing love letters to death
But they all keep getting marked return to sender
I'll keep my distance and walk to the light
I'll close my eyes and pray for sleep this night
I've been writing love letters to death
But she doesn't seem to hear me
I'll close my eyes tight
And pray she's nowhere near me.
I've been writing love letters to death
But she's not listening
I'm done writing
I'm ready to live.

-Stan Lake

My Addictions

I breath heavy
Sucking in the harsh
Dry air of this emptiness
Surrounded by
All the familiar faces
Yet no one I know
They not knowing me
I'm hidden by
My empty soul
Pushing and pushing
To finally be free
My secrets still hidden
For only me
Trusting myself
Myself alone
The only way to be
I keep my door locked
For safety
To be secure
The air in here
Hard to swallow
But worth the
Lack of pain
That fills your heart
I'm not coming out
Not worth the time
Not worth the dead end
For that's all there is
Let me be
Let me be
Let me be
You'll only be happy
By staying away from me
I'll fill your heart with sorrow
And your head with misery

-Branden Ray

-In Love-

Devil's Brew

In a slumber for far too long
Truth was suppressed by a demons song
Cast me out to make me new
Cast me out to make me new
Decipher as to what's right and wrong
Deep down, you've known this all along
Don't drink the devil's brew
Don't drink the devil's brew
He will be your friend,
A false heaven send
Your vision will skew
Your vision will skew

He will build you up,
Your ego is fed
If only you could see
If only you could see
You've been left for dead,
You've lost your head

But what about me?
Hear my song of plea!
I was blind, but now I can see!
This isn't me!
This isn't me!
Lost to the drift,
deep in the abyss
For all is dark and hope is lost
I need the light, no matter the cost

-Barrett McCulloch

Maybe You're Mine

You were born in the month of June
that I know is true.
To a mom and a dad who would raise you right
but wait, there's more.
Because nine months before
me and your mother shared a passion filled night
but alas mom claimed him not me.
I should feel glee and cheer
but when I saw your picture of you, my maybe son
all my heart felt was sorrow and despair.
Because maybe you're mine
and maybe like your father, I'm like mine...

-Dwight Buchanan

That Sweet Thief

a sonnet on motherhood in the military

Buttoned-up battle dress from top to toes;
Hair pulled so tightly temples start to ache.
The lump in my throat telling all my woes;
Left home early before baby could wake.
Heartsick tears leave a bitter aftertaste.
Breast pump billeted in my chem gear bag;
Breastmilk stains on my boots, no time to waste.
This small sacrifice to honor our flag.
Nana called, baby won't take a bottle,
But mission briefings need my attention.
Sleep deprived, can't keep pace at full throttle;
Rank suffers, promotion in suspension.
Service before self sometimes hurts like hell;
The knife cuts deeper with every farewell.

-Robin Ludwig

That Bitch, Death

Death is a person.
She lingers and languishes around begging for attention.
She speaks with tracer rounds on the 1's and the 5's.
She daily clings close and I can't seem to shake her.
Left right left right left right her influences march through my brain.
She lures men to join her never to again be among the living.
Shades wandering about guided by Virgil in those rings of hell.
She flows like a severed femoral artery
And in less than 3 minutes she drains the life force out of once vibrant
men.
Her stains pattern the sand, bloody reminders of what once was.
The tormentor of sleep, the hijacker of my waking hours.
She lures men to their graves and takes great pleasure in a job well done.

-Stan Lake

-In Love-

Illustrator: Justin Craine

My Friend, Fiend

Dr. Faust what is the remedy to life?
You who had a friend and foe in Mephistopheles.
I'll recite to you a similar tale of my own;
Yet, I recognized this devil too late, in my home.

He was a courageous man, attending to wounded on the battlefield;
The Greco-Romans called upon Asclepius (god of medicine), we call our
doc;
Brothers bonded by tragedy and blood, no other more real;
You, valiant fighter and savior of life and limbs, is it here that our hearts
rot?

The burning and screaming are now nostalgic for us;
The doors to my home are flung open for you—my *friend*.
Like a snake who uses another's burrow
So did you, come and bequeath to my bedroom chamber, sorrow.

A spectacle of both me and her were made;
Another typical young military couple fallen prey.
The thirst was too real, a cuckold I'm made
Three Jodys, one marriage, countless photos, videos, messages on instant
replay.

It was not enough to aid *the* half-dead was it doc?
The remedy was to take another's and make it yours.
To feel a *whole* body in your arms: legs, thighs, back and breast.
Your redemption: warm, body-parts in place, nothing missing, that's
your taste.

For the ones you saved have left; but the ones we lost are nested in our
brains.
Fool is the man who leaves his food uncared for,
Who doesn't scan for the vultures of the Earth and sky
I laud you doc, friend of mine, you're the one I'll call upon when *my* life
is on the line.

-Moises Machuca

-In Love-

Honor

Honor—yeah, I know Honor.
He is a man I met late in life.
"Late" as it means to the long-lost teen,
From soil so honorless rife.

Grandaddy clung to the underbelly,
American Dream ripping flesh from the palm.
Grandaddy was a train-hoppin' bandit,
Who I said fought in Vietnam.

Yeah, Honor—yeah, I know Honor.
The streets once so cruel and glum.
The rooms too—bare,
Not a gilded warmth to share,
Just a ruckus in grand maelstrom.

Daddy was a big, bold lover,
Just of the bottle—cold and warm.
Laid flat on floors, this big, bold lover;
Who I said died in Desert Storm.

At the end of the line a lil' early,
Too early, Mama's preacher said.
From the depths beat that ancient billowing drum,
And under warrior's wings I fled.

Pulled—one day,
Or pushed, I could declare,
Many faces now proud,
One silence now loud,
Met me, this Honor so rare.

Here tonight I look upon you,
Seasoned faces; gilded as if divine.
Here tonight I cave and embrace thee,
Truly, fathers and brothers are mine.

-David Rose

The Guard

A reference to controlled violence
It was a reckoning
Proliferating frustration and fear
Armed for this quasi-battle
Bringing a full heart
Smashed and bound
Touching down, in a hubristic stance
Cloaked in armor, gouged and scarred
Close encounters with no holds barred
Fast like a predator, a hunter
Hunting heads
Killing metaphors with snot bubbles and fog
Shock and awe
Penetration through holes that open up with choreography
I fuck that hole with all my fury and revel at the chaos that ensues
I plug it up with barbarity and spew arrogance
I stand in this arena while spectators spectate
I live the love of Art and War and all of its allure

-Nick Misiano

-In Love-

First & Last [Love]

Figuratively speaking,
I've literally died for you.
When I said, "I do"
I was no longer me.
I became we…
Wholeheartedly.
If done haphazardly,
it's a dangerous walk down the aisle.
And the scale will tip towards
the strife between my desires or your
adoration.
A heart's ablation
forces a set of hands to choose:
hold onto convictions, but
at the cost of something to lose.
The crux of Free Will
hangs from the lowest limb, but
Love and Sacrifice
break the curse of original sin.

-Tyler James Carroll

In Love... &War

By age ten I'd killed a thousand men
rifle in hand, bang bang.
"I got you."
"No way, try again."

Call it a rehearsal, a rock drill,
grenade pins in teeth, we took the hill
behind the house
we learned to crouch
and acquire a target behind cover,
the blood, we saved that for later.

War was a game we played.
Joy was the day it rained,
low crawling in the mud like real commandos,
the ones we watched last night on TV
fighting for country
with honor,
duty sacred.
We watched again in the AM,
red and blue lasers never hit the enemy directly
but we know Joe got his man. Joe always wins.
Just like us, the good guys-
The ones killing for the right reasons.
What were those reasons again?
Oh yeah, freedom.

Killing was a game we played,
Subtle was the day that changed.
Amy was her name.
Soft curves sat beneath bold brown eyes,
the days we spent, reliving our nights.
Phoenix in flames prepared to take flight
in a dress made of sun.
It was love while it was fun,
but like all things that aren't love,
this we came undone.
It was time to play again,
a game with no end.

Marching was the game we played
day after day after day in the rain.
Punch, stab, shoot, kick.
Reload the clip.
Pull the pin with your teeth.
"It's not called a clip, asshole.
It's a magazine. Now beat your face."
"Did you just pull that pin with your teeth?
Get the fuck down, Private."
This game plays on and on
long after the fun has gone.
The cycle repeats.

Call of Duty was the game we played.
Ironically, returning to red and blue lasers,
following sullied summer nights like a period
at the end of the abbreviated sentence of our youth.
Burning human flesh, that smell will forever linger.
A simple motor skill, to squeeze the index finger
leaving chunks of brain on a plaster wall,
mixed with fragments of another human's skull.
Watch your step, there's guts on the floor.
Remember last night, they were slippery as hell.
We watched the commander fall in a hole filled with shit.
It was a nice change of pace to laugh for a bit.

Killing was the game we played
and we played it well,
medals we earned from a time spent in hell.
Like family those men became-
like a love untamed- like a willingness to do the same.
To live, to die, to fight and defend
a friend, a brother, a bond with no end.

You see,
infatuation is an old pineapple grenade,
often wounding in a superficial way.
Love is a suicide vest strapped to a zealots chest
hell-bent on destruction and gore.
It's no surprise at all why we fell so deep In Love…

                                                              -Leo Jenkins

-&WAR-

Wicked Profession

Gear check, comm check, press check
Eyes, lights, sights
Pre-dawn insert
In'jin country
Silent nighttime trek

Past the river
Down the wadi
Green cratered moonscape
Single file down
Empty alleys
Through the compound gate

Build the hide site
Frigid cold
Long guns on the roof
Poncho liners
Piss in bottles
Muddy frozen boots

Sun is rising
Crack door open
Peek over the wall
Bazaar filling
Up with people
Prayers are being call'd

Signal picked up
Target moving
Slew drone sensors west
Triangulate
Disseminate
Alert the QRF

Light brown man dress
Jet black turban
'cross the wadi now
Talk the hogs on
Twist the turrets
Crosshairs on his brow

On the bridge
It's now or never
Pull the slack out slow
First round rings out
Sky rips open
Three more fast in tow

Judge and juror
Execution'rs
Death by firing squad
Head split open
Brains are scattered
Sent off to his god

Throw our plates on
Sprint to kill zone
Cordon off far side
Search the body
Transmit pictures
Shit, this ain't our guy

Crowd is gath'ring
Break down hide site
Trucks are round the bend
Move to extract
Home by lunchtime
Warm and safe again

Mission debrief
Intel updates
Target still alive
Lucky bastard
Back to planning
We'll get him next time

In the street
A fam'ly mourning
Borne into this hell
But can we feel bad
That we can kill so well?

-Bryan Crosson

Share What You Can

"I drew a scene of a cat tap dancing."
"What do you mean?"
"What do you mean, what do I mean? It's a cat tap dancing. His shoes
are ruby red with specks of green."

"What the fuck does that have to do with anything?"
"Well, I didn't know how to draw six men standing tall,
Before the blast, before the fall,
Of two fathers, six sons, a newborn ghost.
I can live those things in lucid dreams,
Second squad's alpha and bravo teams, disappearing;
The displaced head of a man, mostly intact,
But I can't share all that, so here's a cat, tap dancing,
His shoes are red and green."

-Leo Jenkins

Joyriding With Kahn

All the hype about the World War Two-ers,
But if Grossman's right; half weren't much doers.
Half!
Half, shootin' their gun;
Joyriding with Kahn, and havin' that fun.
Tougher than their damn hippy kid,
But when Nam came callin, flower-baby flipped a lid,
To get out there, shootin', under the green,
In stench and the blackness, in stench and the steam.
Joyriding with Kahn, brass falling to feet,
And when the Gee-Watt hit, their son's instinct complete:
To kill, to shoot, to see that fucker fall,
To gleam with high-fives in that glorious maul.
Only ones not shootin'—sat, sour as lime,
Were in the wrong place—and at the wrong time.
All this talk about castrated Generation Z,
But Good Old Induction, well, she's callin' to me;
As our people weaken, she says, our fighters grow few,
But Arminius' blood still boils the brew.
Less and less warriors, but better warriors will hatch,
Out of savage wombs, to sprint towards their match.
Joyriding with Kahn, maybe even one day just one,
A lone maverick exiled,
A war just begun.
On a new planet, killing what he can find,
While reading the great epics of the Tora Bora,
The long-outlawed U F C,
And dead deeds of his kind.

-David Rose

Battleship

Boots-deep in jet grease
I was
Digging around in bad circuitry
My brain was
Floating around the Persian Gulf
We were
Watching sailors play war games on a warship—Call of Duty
Was it?
I was
Wondering why the real thing wasn't good enough.

-Laura Hamlet

Back to Babylon
(Originally published in *Ghosts of Babylon*)

The night is deep and warm and black
Our bus pulls slowly across the tarmac
The C-17 sits on the limitless track
Preparing to depart

There are no crowds, speeches or parades
But we wouldn't have it any other way
Just a quiet departure at the end of the day
When we fly into the night so long

The flight into the night that is endlessly long
Tonight we fly to Babylon

Back again to those nights under the thousand and one stars
Stars as bright as the eyes of Ishtar
Like white drops from a giant scimitar
That has cleft the green-black sky

I sling my pack and M4
Moving slowly towards that metal door
Back to where I was before
Back to the dawn of time

The engines emit a humming whine
We circle around the jet turbines
And in a file we shuffle and silently climb
Onto the waiting bird

Not a word is spoken as we climb aboard
Everyone lost in their own private world
The jet races down the track and into the sky is hurled
And we are gone into the night

Moving on towards the early morn
Ahead so many tasks for us to perform
A silent ship of souls we are carefully borne
On to the impending dawn

The dawn that dawned for countless years
Over an antique land of prophets and seers
Beyond our lowering ramp it will appear
In the pink and reddening dawn

The dawn of the days that are so hot and so long
The dawn of days in Babylon

Everyone is sprawled on the floor in a heap
Lost in their own drug-induced sleep
I can't read or rest or think of anything deep
As we fly across the sea

I've lost all conception of time and space
Moving along in some mindless race
Back to the ancient and ancestral place
Back to the land of two rivers

Back again to those historic places
The land of sand and green oases
Working again in the dark and twilight spaces
And we fly towards the dawn

Towards that dawn we're moving on
Moving on to Babylon

Back to those nights so sultry and warm
That bore us like riders on a mechanical storm
Green lasers and shadows like shape-shifting forms
Through the nights that were so black

Those nights that were black as the eyes of an eidolon
Those nights of nights in Babylon

I'm alone in a ship with a hundred men
My thoughts are here, then there, and now and then
Wondering who, and how, and if, and when
I'll have someone to tell me goodbye

The ramp will open and the smell will flood over us
That smell of sewage, burning trash, and dust
There to greet us as we descend to the waiting bus
There to welcome us home

Home again to the river's eternal shore
The land of gods, kings, heroes, and whores
We won't look back when we pass through this golden door
Beyond the far horizon

That lies like a prize beyond the far horizon
Here in the gardens of Babylon

Everyone is sore from the night on the floor
We walk stiffly from the bird's metal door
And we wander like survivors on the Ninevehan shore
Who have been cast from a great Leviathan

Like survivors cast from a great Leviathan
Here unto the shores of Babylon

Lying on my bed inside that great concrete fence
Riding out those nights of aching emptiness
In my music my heart beating that same cadence
It will all be over before long

Everything will end before very long
Just like the glory of Babylon

Here I am for the next hundred days
On to wherever my destiny lays
Cloaked in the sun's blinding rays
And the cold white embrace of the moon

The moon that shines over the Nahr al-Furat
Weaving its way from the slopes of Ararat
Through this land of palaces, hovels and ziggurats
As it has for the past thousands of years

And beneath its waters so murky and deep
So many secrets it surely must keep
The centuries of sediments have buried them heaped
In the banks of this ancient river

It's long past midnight and I'm high over the ocean
Floating on waves of my own emotions
Would that there were someone to receive my devotions
Well, maybe some other time

For now, I'll just sit here feeling this song
Feelings so full, they can't be wrong
The hum of the engines is steady and strong
As they carry me ever on

On and on and on and on
Taking me back to Babylon

-Jonathan Baxter

Moving Out, Moving On

And I still miss the sound of helicopters

sitting in the door, legs over the side
through the night, just living the ride

shoulder to shoulder with my brothers' armor
riding down the sky beneath the rotors' thunder

Riding down the sky with you, my brother

and there was no night too dark for us then
no valley of the shadow too low for us to descend

like the wrath of some biomechanical god

When we were the vanguard of the storm
harbingers of the god of war

and witnesses to the awe

of those precision bombing runs
and the orgasmic bursts of the miniguns

Looking up to watch the tracers slowly arc
ahead of the machine guns' steady bark

crossing the sky like a stream of red ejaculate

and beyond, twinkling in their mystery so high
the thousand stars against the green-black sky

Shooting stars leisurely overhead
as you chased down some raghead

hot and sweaty in your exoskeleton

and already those memories are so distant to me now
like shadows somewhere far beyond tracer burnout
fading, and now gone
like the spent brass cartridge casings I left like those parts of myself
on that ridge, that field, that draw

Moving out, I'm walking point on a one-man patrol
onward to a place that maybe one day I'll know

Alone and onward to the dawn
but I suppose life is all about moving on

The team I left behind is getting ready tonight
to go carry out dark acts in the black of night

Putting on body armor and heading out to the birds
to try to find some bloody equilibrium in this world

and I'm just sitting at a white and black computer screen
writing out memories that were black and green

riding out another night to the dawn

And I'll always miss the sound of helicopters

-Jonathan Baxter

Am I The Enemy Now?

I never pulled my trigger.
I choked on the hair drier heated Iraqi dust
I smelled the shit and diesel burning in the acrid air from the discomfort
of my Humvee
but I never fired a round.
Not even once.
Was I the enemy or were the people of Iraq?
How do I tell?
Are those people in the car approaching our convoy confused citizens of
this desert hell
or are they intent on hurting me?
Should I shoot?
Can I engage?
How will I know?
Maybe I'll throw a rock and if they keep coming then I'll shoot.
Their windshield shattered.
Ok they stopped.
Whew that was close.
Am I the enemy now?

-Stan Lake

Razor's edge

We stand on the thin edge of civil men and savages.
We let out a guttural roar as we sprint towards victory or Valhalla.
We all made the choice to be either man or beast in the arena of battle.
Men of compassion we once were. Hearts and souls now lost, never to
find their way back into our scarred chest.

-Nicholas Rossin

The Patrol

Imagine driving down a very long, straight highway now devoid of life. The landscape is flat, not a rise or dip as far as the horizon. Neat lines of broken metal hulls flank either side of the road, the steel shine of their surfaces dulled by the wind welted sand. It is a graveyard of the beaten and once proud, their twisted bodies still staring into the distance from which you came. They had been waiting for something and it had come, sweeping through far faster and stronger than they had imagined.

No lights shine in the evening dusk but a flickering orange glow pervades the scene casting shadows, locked in a macabre mazurka, on the road and surrounding desert. You can see the sources far off, either side of the road and to your front. They flare angrily, spitting flames, wounded and suffering, calling out in vain for help.

As you speed along all is silent but for the warm wind whipping at the material covering your face and the urgent whine of your engine. Nobody talks; they stare to their sides half-looking for a lingering, uncertain threat, half wondering what had happened in this unhappy place.

The living had been here once; it is hard to tell how long ago. You wonder where they had gone. Tracks in the ground are still visible as if the wind and sand wanted them remembered; you wonder who made these? This lifeless plain heard laughter once, where are those jokers? Whose hands steered the machines and revved their engines?

Are they long dead or are their fresh corpses hidden by the creeping night? Do their families still wail? Do they smile out of frames on a faraway wall, looked at once a year by a remarried wife?

You hope they ran away before it came to them.

The wind blows too fast for the lingering stench of death and you are grateful for the ignorance.

In the middle distance great hulking caverns loom. They too are dark and broken. As you pass you can see each is punctured, the innards spill out of their hastily assembled mouths; concrete intestines, livers and lungs. Their structures are alien to you; tall halls shaped like a letter "A" useless now. You doubt if anyone would return here.

You have passed through the other side, the same road but now nothing either side of you as the hum of the tyres rolls you closer to the flames. They hold your attention, blinding you in the night. A sticky sweet smell greets you, offered in cloying waves by the wind, accusing:

"You did this."

-Neil MacKinnon

Odes to the GWOT

Here stands in the face of unprecedented transition
Testament to unchanging resolve
For which these warriors will be forever known.

Cities were our fought-for islands,
Desert and mountain, rather Grandfather's shores.
A nation asked and thus was answered:
Our bravest men for its longest wars.

-David Rose

The Assaulters
(Originally published in *Ghosts of Babylon*)

the assaulters lounge
sprawled languidly in the oppressive heat
like so many hunting dogs

on the Stryker's ramp
relaxed, our heads back against the door frame
muscles charged with latent energy

leaning back in our kits
we sit, helmets off, radio traffic
idly crackles in the background

waiting on THE WORD

rifle muzzles down
hands contouring down lower receivers
fingers curved over triggers

the metal ramp is littered
bottles filled with dip spit collect
like the sunflower seeds at our boots

we're territorial like that

the conversations flow
the profanity spoken like poetry
pungent punctuation marks

pop pop pop
dip can coming out of shoulder pocket
communion plate passed around

the raunchiest stories ever
war obscenities, sexual outrages
the funniest stories you ever heard

outbursts of laughter
like the dip spit spilling out from our lips
"you cannot make up this shit!"

walk away from the group
to piss by the tombstones, return again
to resume staining the dust with spit

and the laughter is
an affirmation, group absolution
more sacred than could come from a priest

"I get it, dude. That's fucked up, and you're fucked up,
but I get it because I'm fucked up too."

and you'll never be alone
so long as we're here with you
on this Stryker ramp
here in this graveyard
somewhere in Babylon

and like that the moment is passed
as the WORD descends like the Hand of God
Launch or RTB

we put our MICHs on
and cram back into our metal cocoons
never to return to that moment

it briefly hangs behind us
over the sunflower seeds and dust stains
before slowly fading away

some of us move on
we make some attempts to remain in touch
but it will never be the same

not like it was back then

some of us try to settle
into the REAL WORLD, where we try to speak
a new language unstained by tobacco

or dead baby jokes
where civilians measure your cock by your
salary, car, or social status

and not by your competence
or by how well you shoot or by the
weights you can throw around in the gym

or that certain assurance
in your voice as you cross that last threshold
into that yawning and hungry darkness

lit only by your taclights

"Need one!"
"Got one!"
Touch.
Entry.
"Clear."
"Clear."

assimilating into
a world where the friendships are measured in
the affectations of affability

not in the burden of shared misery
Ft. Benning in the dark before the dawn
another platoon formation run

around the airfield
carrying forty pound water jugs then
buddy-carries up Cardiac Hill

the Legs look at us
furtively, like domestic animals
eyeing a wolfpack stealing by

halfway point
you carried me, now I will carry you
to the top of this damn hill

we assimilate
keeping lonely midnight vigils as we
make myths out of our memories

as we relive the past
looking at the photos, raising a glass
consecrated to those passed

and failing to adjust
going back to the closest thing we can find
wearing civvies this time

and slinging up our rifles
we go seeking the warrior culture
trying to find the past in the future

we return again
to the land we left where we try to find
that which we left behind back there

trying to find that moment again

but the only ones
who never truly left that moment were
the ones who joined with it forever

in an instant's flash
in the crushing overpressure or in
a single shot in a darkened room

or the ones who dived
into a substance-abuse death spiral
or health crisis or car crash

they left the moment
only to become one with it later
in another time and place

these are the only ones forever in the moment now

we drink to it
dream of joining it, give it labels like
Valhalla, Hall of the Slain

but it's back there
in that old, dusty Ramadi graveyard
the rooftops and the airfields

back there in the places
where we bided our time in the moments
that we shared and that defined us

-Jonathan Baxter

The OPTEMPO was high in cities like Ramadi prior to the 2007 Al Anbar Awakening. Many of our missions would be against time-sensitive targets. There was one old graveyard out in the city where our platoon would stage our Stryker vehicles and loiter, waiting for the launch command.

Illustrator: Justin Craine

Overhead

Rounds snap overhead.
Marines bleed, and wounds get aid.
Nine-line for the dead.

-Justin Eggen

Nightfall

Nightfall goons come out.
Moving in silence we prowl...
NODs drop on my scowl.

-Justin Eggen

No Politics

Triggers are pulled on the exhale,
The bolt ejecting the brass. "They're right out in front!" Shouts the
Marine in the grass. Rounds impacting all around, Fiercely snapping
past.
The fight just got real—
Marines digging into position.
We've prepared for this.
We're incredibly efficient—
240s and 40 mike mike
SAWs and 5.56.
Down here in the dirt there are no politics.

-Justin Eggen

GWOT TrapLordz OEF

31 North and 63 East—
This is where you'll find our clarity increased. Helmand Valley Gun
Club is a brotherhood of warriors, from Now-Zad, Marjah, and Sangin
our battlefields are notorious.
Close the feed tray cover and rack it back twice. Adjust the T&E whilst
aiming down the sights. Murkin in Marjah or Bangin in Sangin,
Every single step we're sweeping and clearing. BIPing IEDs while
shooting tow missiles
When IDF comes, you'll hear the whistle. HIMARS all day flying high
in the sky,
While everyone is watching, we're taking
shit from supply.
We're the GWOT TRAPLORDZ; Pop smoke on that wall charge—
We're not taking the door

-Justin Eggen

IEDs

It's loud.
The pressure is paralyzing.
My flak compresses my spine;
The pressure squeezes my mind.
Noise turns to silence as my ears mute the racket. Nothing can prepare
you—
No form of practice.

-Justin Eggen

Not Today

It's so loud I forget who I am. I can't feel anything; I can't hear anything.
I try to open my eyes. I cannot see anything; my body is in shock.
"Not today."
Something loud has happened, something abrupt. My life will never be
the same. I know that instantly. What has happened? Where am I? Why
am I here? What the fuck is happening?
"Not today."
You will not meet Death today. Not today, not tomorrow. You may go
through loss. You will see horrors... but you will not experience Death....
"Not today."
I gather myself.
I'm standing two meters away from the blast site. I look around the area.
I feel the sun, I smell the air, I see my boys...
Not today, Motherfucker.

-Justin Eggen

Compassion Lost

Our packs are heavy, but we don't complain, Patrolling through marijuana fields, all types of strains. Forever we fight, strong and resilient.
You'd be surprised that our enemies are brilliant. Building new bombs every single day. Emplacing them in all the pathways,
Forever adapting to our tactics—
We find their bombs with months and months of practice.
We train our eyes, and our eyes don't deceive.
So when you find something, you don't disbelieve.
You go with your instincts to stay alive...
In this dangerous game it's the only way to survive. Once you've become complacent, you're lost. You're useless to everyone- you've become soft. Marines here are hard chargers who fight for fun. We're fierce Devil Dogs who refuse to get overrun. Taking the fight to the enemy relentlessly, Decisions are always right, incidentally.
In combat there is no questioning,
Only actions.
Over time you lose all compassion.

-Justin Eggen

Illustrator: Justin Craine

The Indifference

This room, where
allies become Taliban,
where the care is bitter,
languages pass one another,
turning an ally, a sympathizer,
into the hate-filled, jihad-obsessed;
the silent broken moments in this room,
when the interpreters are on a smoke break,
or just not present to explain to those bedridden
why one of their own cries in pain as we move him.

We need to clean him, rotate him to prevent bedsores,
prevent him from hurting himself any further,
administer treatment to help him heal—
it will hurt like hell while performed;
but they only hear the loud cries,
only see us struggle with him,
see him struggle with us,
crying out to Allah,
to the tajiman*,
to them.

-Curt Last

*Afghan for 'interpreter'

TIC

It's hard to describe how sounds can be angry,
But these were the sounds of hate, and they had soft destinations.

Naivety was dragged away in full view, unsalvageable-
Like the light of a sinking vessel, disappearing beneath the waves.

The symphony of steel raged, unconcerned.
This was the devil's domain, and we were welcome guests.

-Mac Caltrider

Sonnet 1

Oh doc, did you perchance encounter fiends
In battlefields where blood allegiance made
Across the plain hollow burning men scream
They call for you to blow them out, to save

A real hero no! Rescued one's life
You ran and picked the littered limbs there thrown
To me, another mode to live, is strife
Those healing hands preserving heart and bone

But still, to whom does this all matter to?
When virtue overseas came home a vice.
In secret places laid bride and you
Three mangled bodies here; you rape what's mine.

If we do meet again before the end,
Your name and fame, remember, bring you shame.

-Moises Machuca

The River Valley

Their blood ran red
In the river valley they bled

Fields of poppy, smoke and stone
Trudging with packs eerily alone

Into the darkness green glow abound
Closing the compound not even a sound

A flash in the dark
A scream in the night

Their blood ran red
In the river valley they bled

Standing their ground
Heat rising around

A whiz and a crack
Chaos pierced the flak

A story cut short
A mother who hurts

Their blood ran red
In the river valley they bled

Dirt and debris obscured the hurt
Empty magazines on the dirt

Helo inbound echoing sound
Slowly draping the mound

One less than they started
A brother departed

Their blood ran red
In the river valley they bled

-Kellen Gumm

Haji #1

Run and run, through the cold dark,
You think we're blind, you think we can't see
But we are not human, Devils we be.
Our wide green eyes pierce the night sky,
You think you're smart, you think sublime.
Ignoring the signs this war has shown,
Our strength and skill will shortly be known.

Pupils wide … heart stopped…

Strings of green pierce the thin black air,
The space on your chest, our lasers share.
Click click go the triggers, a symphony of sound,
You are the first Haji I've seen shot down.

Heavy sigh of… relief

-Zack Shier

Faithless in the Fog of War

I'm a heretic and a hypocrite
Carrying the weight of the world
And memories I can't seem to forget
I over analyze the trauma forevermore
When will the horrors of war not plague me anymore
I close my eyes
I see the man I used to be
The blood on the pavement
The pressure not to just lament
The burden of a heavy heart
The hopelessness of being worlds apart
I shake my fist at the sky
Come down and save me
Show me the love they preach about
Come down to this combat zone
Where there's no love to be shown
Show me who you are
Reach down and save me
Bring me out of the depths
Oh death where is your victory
Where is your sting
You have been defeated
I'm still fucking breathing.

-Stan Lake

The Death Of The Humvee Turret Gunner

From my mother's embrace I rose to the call of the State,
And I hunkered in its steel until my dry skin melted.
Six hundred meters from base, I shuffled off this mortal coil;
I fell asleep to the sound of exploding copper. No more nightmares.
At "end of mission," they flushed me out of the turret with a hose.

-Charles Faint

Everyday Fallujah

Pardon thee as we burst into flames
The AKs and RPGs are calling our names
Open your eyes and witness what they see
An ominous landscape of never-ending calamity
This place is poisoned, rotting from inside
A fanatical ideology from which no one can hide
Born into a side and hold on for the ride
Material has degraded to its truest form
Reality is weathered by the torrential storm
Structures fall to rubble, the hair on their faces begins to stubble
When hajji comes to play, there's gonna be trouble
Put a round into his head and bust his bubble
Inhaling cigarette smoke and Composition B
No laws, no remorse, nor morality
Our habits are destructive, deliberately
Caught in the perils of the fight to be free
Look through a different pair of lenses to see
There is no life without the possibility of an opportunity
All that remains are the instinctive survivors
The swift, elusive, terrorist connivers
Dog and cats eating human cadavers
The evil city of Hell on the Euphrates
No coins for enemy eyes while crossing Hades
The crescent of a once thriving, fertile land
Damned to the cold, darkness, dust, and sand

-Nick Misiano

Chow Conversation

Sat down for morning chow,
a long night shift over, the stumble
down the dirt roads of KAF
as it just starts to heat up at 0700.
The base quiet, the dust laid,
past the Boardwalk to the National DFAC
where I see HM1 Mursky—
a buddy who works in our blood lab,
and he actually invites me
to sit down—me, the most unapproachable
enlisted service member at Role 3,
but we go back to indoc
at Port Hueneme—where this all
started for us.

"Last, you missed it yesterday,"
he says in his nasal,
always-trying-to-find-the-humor
in-stupid-military-bullshit-way,
and he just loves the way
I roll my eyes
whenever policy and procedure
pile up to embrace the suck,
or whatever new events
at the hospital defy logic,
or are just completely insane.
"Why, what's up?" I raise
from my monotone,
to accentuate my eternally sardonic voice.
"We had a really bad call,
some Marines came in with IED
injuries. This one had his legs
and an arm blown off.
The doc on duty asks him,
'Are you ok?' and he says,
'What do you mean,
am I ok?? I only have one arm!"

There's a chuckle,
and I chuckle. It's that darkness—
the brute honesty that attacks
a question that is truly
insane, yet a requirement
in order to process patient cognition.

It's when protocol goes
out the window,
when an enlisted can basically
tell an officer to "FUCK OFF!"
and fuck off with righteousness,
knowing nothing can be lost.
It's the cruel ridiculousness
of what we see almost every day
coming into the hospital,
or residing in it until death
or some almost happy ending
do we part with patient,
though where they come from
tells a lot about their chances.

In the case of locals,
some have a slow death in our ICU.
In the case of our troops,
often a long flight to Lundstuhl,
followed by a longer flight
home... a bed at Walter Reed
or Bethesda down the street.
But me and HM1 Mursky,
we can only chuckle
at all of the insane bullshit—
we've been here months
and have months to go.

-Curt Last

Dead Haji

Like a dog you died
You were killed and thrown aside
Mouth agape and rigor mortis set
You lay stiff-legged straight
On the side of the highway
Eyes wide arms straight
Lying, watching, you wait
Were you screaming
You look like you're screaming
Eyes wide arms straight
Rigor mortis mouth agape
Why did they kill you?
Why were you thrown aside?
On the highway we found you
Like a dog you died

-Stan Lake

-&War-

...Of Life and Death

We have been infused with the thirst for WAR. An addiction for combat. Understand it's not an addiction to killing. It's the thrill of life and death. Not everyone gets to experience this the way we did. Everything is better after. Food, beer, LIFE...but the downfall comes when it all goes bland again. It leaves us wanting more. It leaves us wanting WAR.

-Vincent Vargas

Contract For Suffering

Dedicated to Chuck Palahniuk and Rudyard Kipling

Come with me, if you will,
To a land war-torn and fair,
Too many men, born in Times of Plenty,
Now blades shall cleave the air:

We are poor, dirty, and heathen; our lot,
Will be for all-time—if they have their say.
Three hundred years our 'Pressors—we ain't forgot,
How they slaughtered and pillaged our way.

They killed my granddad, when I was young,
Killed him with a bullet to the brain.
Then punished full; my juvenile tongue,
Bold and boyish, but foolish, I sustain.

But the tides, they are a-changin',
My uncles and brothers, we gather,
We are signing the most ancient of contracts,
Dead and still, than survive, we'd rather.

Come with me, if you will,
To a land war-torn and diseased,
Too many men, born in Times of Plenty,
Now bullets shall cleanse it with ease:

We are iron, focused, and lethal; this group,
Will be for all-time, if we have a say.
We avenge or defend—the whole earth over,
Better meant for a good pillage—but, hey…

Harken here—to the gentler man,
Who'd beg these people reprieved.
Oh, they might be right—and they may be wrong—but they signed the ancient
contract,
One—both sides believe.

Harken here—to the weak of our lot;
Trembling—enemy's noble roar!
You signed the motherfuckin' contract,
From the body, a soul has to soar.

-David Rose

The Gulf

The night was bright as ever.
A full moon hung over the gulf;
an ancient celestial orb.
I myself, struggling.
The wind howling.
Like a song beckoning battle.
As clouds part for a war vessel.
I'm eager to heed a call.
That came in the middle of the night.
I slammed my head as I made way out my rack.
I awoke someone, they murmured some speech I couldn't comprehend.
Half naked, and not a care.
I went up a ladder well;
And down another, my foot getting caught and my boot flying.
I grabbed it and then, in front of the armory I stood.
An ink riddled young man, screaming for the machine gun and
ammunition to boot.

Outside, the wind long dead, and the sea flat as a desert.
I scanned darkly. The moon shrouded by a congregation of clouds. Over
comms, someone made a joke. Some stereotype bullshit. Then Chief
chimed in, told them to *shut the fuck up.*
I stood above a flight deck, where men better than me had repelled onto.
Outward, I looked to the fires on the horizon.
Thin haze, dots of orange against the vast black.
Burning Bright still.
FAC-FIAC outbound.
Another heedless call in a place so desolate.
I question it all;
And remain without an answer.

-Ryan Kisner

God

Oh good! There's the sun. No more night. No more moving through these mountains like blind, drunken men. Now if we get hit we can actually see what we're shooting at. Never understood why they don't kill us. It would be so easy. Oh well, this is the last one. Then it's back home. Cold beer. Warm woman. Beer definitely. Warm woman—bonus. A non-lethal mission. Until it becomes lethal. Here they come. The word's gotten out. The mountain people from another time. How do they live out here? Nothing marks the time besides night and day. They're on their own. Is there such thing as an opinion out here? These mountains don't have an opinion. That's for sure. A still observer. Here, the weak really get rubbed out. That's their fact of life. Back home, they call it the land of the free. Naw, we pay for the concrete, the convenience, the security, the long life. Are these people coming out from behind these rocks the ones who are really free? Huh....

The kids line up quick. They don't look sick to me. They don't want medicine. They want what we got. Maybe some presents. I guess kids are the same anywhere you go. These kids definitely aren't spoiled. Strange, they don't seem neglected either. They're just existing. They don't have to become anything. Only be. I need to take a picture. I know I'll never see this again. Hope it comes out good. Need to invest in a better camera than this cheap, disposable one.

That soldier's a big boy over there. What's up with the burnt orange hair and the white, freckled face? How the hell did he get out here? Usually, I would never ask something like this, but why not? I'll never see this guy again. It's too easy. Our interpreter is standing right next to him.

"Can you ask him why he has the red hair, white skin, freckled face? Just seems out of place for an Afghan mountain soldier."

He's so calm, whatever he's saying. He won't look at me, though. I don't blame him. "If I only knew," is probably what he's thinking.

"He said in the '80s, when Afghanistan was at war with the Soviets, his mother was raped during their breeding-out campaign. That's why he looks the way he does. He's half Russian."

Wow! What do you say to that? Not a whole lot. It already says everything. What does that make me to him? An occupier? A liberator? No matter what, I'm not a rapist trying to wash out a national bloodline. I'd like to think we're here to help. And, of course, gather intelligence.

What's this?

Get at the ready! What's the commotion over there? More people. Suicide bomber in their midst. It could happen. It has happened. A lot. It's always kids, too. All for Allah. How do you fight that? You don't.

Oh, it's a man holding his baby. The baby could be wired. Stranger things have happened. It looks like the baby's sicker than a dog. That's a good sign he's not wired. His dad's bawling his eyes out. I guess I would be, too. Still, have to stay at the ready. It could all be for show. No waiting in line for these two. To the front of the line they go. On past our lazy cordon. They're almost to Doc. Wait for it…wait for it…

No explosion.

Relax.

Now they're getting something simple from us that they just don't have out here. Maybe penicillin? I don't know. I'm not a medic. I'm guessing the baby will live now. That's good. At least this mission wasn't a complete waste of time.

There's the presents! Soccer balls and backpacks. Oh look, Sgt. Gregory, the prick, is human after all. I have to take a picture of this.

Take the ball, kid. It's yours! Hell, take a backpack, too! I know it's the little things when you're dealing with the big things. Everything seems OK now. Everyone seems at ease.

Corporal Klus is sitting down. Well, don't mind if I do. No way to get on my ass if he's doing the same thing. Give my shoulders a rest. This pack weighs a ton. They never said a forward observer would have to carry so much shit. Actually, they said a lot of things and didn't say a lot of things. And here we are. How did that happen?

Aw, quit your bitching. It's like Sgt. Strait said, "If a soldier isn't bitching, he's dead." Just enjoy the downtime in the daytime—safe.

(Half-hour later)

Oh no, Sgt. Strait looks pissed. Never a good thing, and he's coming this way. "Sgt. Gregory, they missed the drop point. The package is on top of the mountain. I need you and another to get up there, pack up as much as you can, and bring it back down here so we can finish the rest of this med-cap and go home."

Oooh, Gregory's not happy about that. Why is he walking over here? "Hey Klus, I need one of your guys."

It's either me or Wagner. I got a bad feeling. "Take Sonnier."

No! Feeding me to the dogs again! Don't worry about me, Klus! You just sit there and take it easy! That's what rank gets you! Can't wait to get mine! Then I can delegate and sit on my ass!

"Let's get up there, Turd!"
Just me and Gregory now.
Ambush.
Turkey shoot.
Too easy.
Where the hell are we going anyway? *They're* always watching us. It's *their* mountains after all. Why don't *they* just kill us? This is such a bad idea. There haven't been a lot of good ones lately. I signed the dotted line, pledged the oath. My fault. Quit bitching. Move forward. Out of my hands.
(Just under an hour later)
"There it is!"
Oh man, it's scattered everywhere. What a mess. What else did I expect?
"Pack up as much as you can. Then we're gone."
We might get half of all this back down. They'll gobble it up in less than an hour. What good is that going to do? It's not worth my life. What if they send us back up? My legs are so smoked. Why are we doing this? Why do I keep on asking that question? It doesn't matter. I just want to go home where life at least makes a little bit of sense. There I go! Bitching again!
(He looks up from the ground)
Oh, look at that! Behold!
Your majesty.
Still.
Timeless.
Never-ending.
The highest point with my feet upon the ground.
I was raised to worship symbols, words, and a God I will never see with my living eyes. This begs new questions. Why did I reach my hands to the sky in a church among fellow God-seekers? Why did I let them dunk my head beneath the water to make me whole again? Why did I fall backward at the faint touch of a man said to be holier than myself? Why did I roll on the ground with all the other fools, laughing my head off, pretending the rivers of joy were flowing from my belly?
It was to feel something.
Something greater.
But it was nothing.
But this!
This is real!

How did it all come to be? The massiveness? The colors? The attention to detail? It all seems to be touched by another.

No concrete. No signs. No blight. Nothing ruined by us…not just yet. I'm not looking down or looking up. I'm looking even.

The sky.

The land.

Me.

We're all the same thing.

No!

Parts of the same thing.

Lost in a dead stare. Who blinks first? I know it's going to be me. I'm so small. So insignificant.

This is God.

The mother.

The father.

The almighty birth.

The longest life.

The living mural.

The natural artist.

The everlasting peace.

I feel I could stay up here forever. In this connection. In this moment.

What could ruin it?

"Hey, Turd!"

There's the answer to my question. It never fails.

But they're not going to take this moment away from me. Once in a lifetime. Burnt into me. Mine!

Will I ever be here again? Around these people from another time? In these mountains of magic? In the thin, crisp air where the night lets every star shine without competition…without selfish human glow?

Never.

Not a chance.

"Put that pack on your back! Back down we go!"

Yep…you're sure right…back down we go.

-Christian Sonnier

It Still Kills

Complacency. Weeks before I drove over and IED, I told people it was gonna happen…even going as far as offering my own time and words to remedy what was brewing, aimlessly pursuing someone that would carry the secondary objective of Marine Corps Leadership in high regard…and it was hard, to keep from literally screaming words like, "You're dreaming if you fail to recognize the disguise of men working hard at hardly working…Staff Sergeant…Sir," because unexplainably dark nights are boring, and complacency kills, when the thrills and nervous energy of war become things you slide off your shoulders and place on the floor, when it's time to literally become your brother's keeper, and not succumb to the dumb idea that a false sense of security is still some type of security. I wonder how they felt, when it happened…and happened, to me, and what came to lie waist high, in front of them…was exactly what I said it would be. If I would have died, I would have predicted my own death, knowingly breathed my last breath…and now I'm left, with an overwhelming sense of disconnect, more often than I'm not, and that spot on my head of smooth baldness, is back – again. When will it end…all of it.

-Emilio Gallegos

Double-Knot

The overpressure hit like the horns of an invisible bull,
Leaving us battered Matadors, with muscles bludgeoned and ribs staved.
Prodded from slumber by the weight of an unsuspecting foot,
A subterranean colossus- Twenty-five pounds of Urea Nitrate.

The moisture, which moments before lubricated my mouth and eyes,
Was yanked away by invisible hands.
All dampness gone in an immeasurably fast instant.

Smoke made the world disappear,
Wrapping itself around my shoulders like some diseased blanket.
The ability to hear was snuffed out,
Replaced by the high-pitched ring of damaged cochleae.

My legs felt like they weren't assembled properly.
Each step tickled with the anticipation of another explosion,
One meant for me.

His laces withstood the force that his body could not.
One leg rode the blast like a perfectly slotted surfer.
The other simply disappeared,
Along with our false sense of invincibility.

-Mac Caltrider

Primary Driver

I drive the primary vehicle, slowly cruise out, watching speed,
and stack up right off the runway, then wait until a visual
is established on inbound Medevac and armed escort. Teams
fall out, sit silently and intent—some joke and salsa dance.

Black dots in the distance—they grow—our two Blackhawks,
I pull onto flight line after our blockers roll out on to the airstrip
to our north and south—Air Force-manned Humvees that ensure
no incoming or outgoing aircraft will interfere with our operation.

I peel in a J shape to a point just outside the big landing X of KILO,
just enough to avoid the helo rotors by 20 meters or so, but close
enough to spare the litter crew the burden of extra steps
with a heavy load and additional seconds wasted carrying too far.

The litter crews jump out, grab sides, brace for the helos' wash,
the other driver and I sit safely in our vehicles, goggles on
to shield eyes from dust, though I keep my helmet on—in case
I'm needed—anything which may call for a change in protocol.

Peering into my side mirror, the litter crew approaches the helo,
wounded pulled out, legs first, walked straight out from Blackhawk's
hatch—avoiding the downward spin of blades—turned and spun toward
Humvee so patient goes in headfirst, the lift of faith, of patient in air.

I pull my body to the right, look inside the rear of my vehicle.
I turn and observe the flight line leader grab the top legs of the litter,
pull the patient up, hobble awkwardly backward. As the rear legs
of the litter slide on rails, he gets down and applies O2 mask.

The PJ jumps in, starts debriefing him, flight line leader goes to work,
gives a thumbs up to me—I pull off the runway, a few small turns,
honk at any traffic or pedestrians, pull up to trauma bay, brake pedal,
apply the emergency brake and put it in park as my engine idles.

The patient is unloaded outside trauma bay, placed on a rickshaw,
secured by clamps, as the master at arms searches through thermal wrap,
clothing, between body and stretcher, making sure there isn't any loose
ordnance that can roll out in our trauma bay and kill one of our teams.

Thumbs up from the MA, two trauma corpsmen waiting inside run out,
kick out the rickshaw legs and roll the patient into the trauma room.
I pull forward, back up with help from a ground guide, over crackling
gravel,
and park my vehicle. My official duty is complete. I grab my cranial,
head back.

-Curt Last

Welcome Home

The banner still hangs limp in the living room or barracks room
screaming
Welcome Home
So why don't I feel welcome?
Home on leave or home at home doesn't feel like home at all.
I feel naked, scared
rifle in the armory, carpet on bare feet expired driver license, new cat,
new chair, new house, my son taller now
nothing the same but I
don't remember seeing any changes.
how could I? I wasn't here.
Welcome home.
I'm too bored, too tired, too excited, too bored, too tired, too anxious
Traffic too fast, bills too due, wife too clingy, family too anxious,
to see me
did you kill anyone, what was it like, I could never, were you scared?
I don't know how to answer.
People close in on me walking by me
Loud restaurants, loud crowds, loud silence
I just want to go back to normal, to rifles and Kevlar and boots and dust
and sweat and generator noise and portashitter and mortar shells and
rockets and arty and small arms and Mesopotamia
Welcome home.

-Michael Ramos

Dissonance

When the dissonance turns to distance and I just can't handle this
When you're supposed to have it all figured out but you can't even get
your own shit together
Breathe in
Breathe out
Sigh
No relief
No hope
No end
Swallow it down
Swallow it down
Bury the pain
Pretend it's OK
Bury it down
No hope here
Just bury it down
You're a man
Be a man
Bury it down
Further
Deeper
Dead.

-Stan Lake

Voices

It was unjust they say. It was all for oil they say. Capitalist, imperialist, some other -ist they say.

That's your right I say. Welcome home they say. You're a hero they say. No I'm not I say. Too long they say. Too expensive they say. Too many they say. You've forgotten the Towers I say. Poor Muslims they say. Murderers they say. Glad they died they say. It wasn't your son I say. Thank you they say. I'll buy you a drink they say. Dinner's on me they say. Thank you I say. I could never serve they say. Never had the opportunity they say. It's all-volunteer I say. Welcome home they say. Proud of you they say. Ashamed of you they say. Afraid of you they say. Won't hire you they say. Don't want a handout I say. It's over they say. It's almost over they say. Forget about it they say. It's history they say.

Tell that to my memories.

-Michael Ramos

-EPILOGUES & EPITAPHS-

Posthumous Self-Indulgent Inquiries in a Final Letter to You, Old Friend.

Was it the first time in a long time you felt warm? A blanket cascade of crimson life, on loan, returning. Fast at first, I'm sure, spurting. When the blood slowed and the warmth turned cold, did you think of them? Your children? What a moment that must have been, did you think you made a mistake? Knowing you can't reach down down down the drain and grab your life again. Cold now. Tired. Did you see the platelets struggling frantically, desperate to keep you together? Did life dry before your wet eyes? Did you know we all cared, no, we loved you and would have done anything to keep your life out of the drain. All of us, the strength, the resilience, what we would've done. Despite our vast reach, we still can't pull your living parts back up now. You're all mixed with piss and shit and shampoo and your daughter's long blonde hair that always clogged the drain. I know, you meant to take care of that last week but didn't get around to it. You were busy. Well, that's what you told us. Really you were in a crippling state of desperate depression, unnecessarily battling alone. We didn't know. You were "too strong" to let on. True strength is asking for help. That's why I don't understand, you were always the strong one. The one we admired. I hope you didn't see your life coating and staining that blonde hair you used to brush. I hope that didn't make you think about her first haircut or the time you were teaching her to ride her bike and she fell off and got that scar on her forehead, the one you used to kiss every night as she fell asleep. No one to kiss away her pain now. I hope you didn't think of all that between the time you opened yourself and when your eyes closed the very last time.

Anyway, tell the other guys I said hello, I love them, and that we are all doing our best to take care of each of your daughters now.

Sincerely,

-Leo Jenkins

Breathe In, Breathe Out

Sit at ease while the people pass.
Their smiles protect others from their depression.
Breathe In, Breathe Out
A sea of people, tides coming & going:
How each life has its waves.
Breathe In, Breathe Out
Confused looks, looking this way & that.
Follow your intuition and you will never be lost.
Breathe In, Breathe Out
I see your eyes. Smile. It's all okay.
Walk tall & walk with pride.
Breathe In, Breathe Out
Let them look, they see you through sleepy eyes.
Let them die, they have committed suicide.
Breathe In, Breathe Out
Breathe In... Breathe Out...

-Daniel Brown

Neuron

Boom, Bang, Boom, Bang, Snap, React
Snap, React
Boom, Bang, Snap, React
Boom, Bang, Snap, React
React, Surge, Boom

Neuron why so clever?
Why so unique?
Your mission to transmit information,
Let's hope the message is received

Boom, Bang, Snap, React
Boom, Bang, Snap, React
Boom, Bang, Snap, React
React, Surge, Boom

Like a tree's roots,
Your dendrites gather vital info
Delivering it to your cell body,
Let's hope this process doesn't blow

Boom, Bang, Snap, React
Boom, Bang, Snap, React
React, Surge, Boom

Axon connection is required,
When there is a second neuron
A synapses is desired
Let's hope the info takes the path most beneficial

Boom, Bang, Snap, React
React, Surge, Boom

Muscles twitch, a migraine follows,
What could these axons be doing?
Something is wrong my brain feels hollow,
Let's hope the cells the axons stimulate are right

React, Surge, Boom

Lucky me the Neuron nucleus contains the best genes,
Stimulate Axon, Simulate Dendrites
Recovery of the cells completes,
Let's hope this function test brings me peace

Info, Processing...Peace

-Daniel Brown

Airway, Breathing, Circulation

Was your last breath a sigh of relief or a gasp for revival?
Either way, it took my breath away.
I screamed your name, shook your shoulders, felt no pulse.
You screamed no pain, shook my existence, felt no more.
Your life flashed before my eyes until my vision went dark.
"I cannot see!" I screamed.
But saw my wife, my mom, and what was about to be my history.
Take a knee. Drink water.
You're losing too much fluids.
Performed a self-assessment during a patient assessment.
Okay.
Time to focus, this isn't how it ends.
And luckily it wasn't.

Years passed by but I became stuck in that moment.
Suffocating, clawing my way out, yet not escaping.
With shallow intentions of superficial affirmation.
"You did all you could."
"It was out of your hands."
I would nod by head, but
think about you're dried blood under my nailbeds.
And then, again, think about your last breath.
Was it a sigh of relief or a gasp for revival?
Either way, it took my breath away.
Until the day I heard my son's first breath.
It's ironic how echoes of pain bring comfort to my ears, because
it signifies life conquering death.

-Tyler James Carroll

-Epilogues & Epitaphs-

The Acceptable Norm

Our war is background noise.
Society pushes on, accepting something is going on, But never fully
understanding that we've all come and gone.
Our forgotten war or the acceptable norm? We've been in combat for
half the time since I was born. In 2001 when our towers were torn, they
were taken from us and we have steadily mourned. Warriors come home,
and no one bats an eye,
but we have lost our friends who now live in the sky.
Everyone doesn't acknowledge the fact that men sacrificed. It seems
almost as if nothing we do will suffice.
People live on with their daily life, never wanting to see the truth beyond
their mind: that young men and women have paid the ultimate price.

-Justin Eggen

A Promise to a Friend

Damn, man, it's great to see you again
I was hoping the last time we talked
Wouldn't be the last before the end
I have so much to say and I'm not sure how long I have to say it

Thank you for making a man out of me
If it wasn't for your leadership, I wouldn't be in this position that you see
You were my mentor, my teacher, my friend
my savior and means to an end—
of an old life that wasn't me
I was immature and not ready for reality

But the lessons you taught I carry with me daily
It's the way I live my life and they've paid off greatly
I want to make a promise to you that you didn't die in vain
I will be successful no matter what, even if it drives me insane

I owe you that much for the things you sacrificed
your family, your kids, and even your life
Imagine how vulnerable we felt to lose a man of your class
Wasn't something we were trained to do, no matter how much time might
pass

But I am getting strong with more time that goes by
Even if I sometimes fear I might forget about you
If I don't acknowledge the anniversary of when you died

I not sure what you want me to do
Can I get some advice? Maybe a hint or a clue
I need to know it's OK to move on
I can't let that day kill me the way it did you...

...because if I do, then those bastards got me, too

I refuse to let you die in vain
I will keep pushing to be successful until it drives me insane
Sorry, I am talking off your ear
There is just so much I want to tell you
So much I need to get clear

What was that? You want to know how your family has been?
Oh, they've been good, man
From time to time the boys and I check on them
Little Jonny's playing baseball now and has a great swing
A real natural, you know
You should see him now. He is getting so big
But you'd recognize his smile; it's like a carbon copy of you as a kid
When he is with his friends he has the same laugh you did

Your daughter, Victoria, she is dating now
I know, I know it isn't how
It's been seven years, and she's 16 now
Don't worry too much, brother
We always have close sight
She's a good kid, man, you raised her right

How's Kelly? Well she remarried last year.
He's a police officer, not a Ranger.
It's nice to see Kelly's no longer a single mother
He treats the kids good, but not sure if you want to hear
They have their own child now
His name is Hunter and he is almost a year

I think It's good to see them live
They were so lost for some time
and something had to give

Come to think of it, I should take my own words to heart
Because life since you left? I haven't let it start
They moved on, and I think it's time I do, too

Thank you for your guidance and for your family's strength
Gone but never forgotten
Thank you for your sacrifice, it won't be in vain
I will start living this life that I have been given
Thank you for visiting me in my dream
Thank you again and again.

-Vincent Vargas

To Whom it Concerned

Imprinted faces with no names
I, the custodian of your graves
Address you—could I?
On cemetery bed, head lays
Polluted pool of life

Surplus imagination
Limbless and formless body
The womb-tomb destination
Left your future to guessing
Perverted pool of life

We never met, me and you
Better to die before you live too—
Could you have been the ubermensch?
Cobwebs decorate your unmarked tombs
Polemic pool of life

Weightless in my arms
Swaying on my conscious-noose tied-tight
Heirloom missing charms
No identity found
Posthumous seed with no life

Gate shutters, maid spring-cleans
Room for weeds to grow with infant-trees.

-Moises Machuca

Fixing an Old Saw

Old saw you, from where did you come?
How many calloused hands held you through a day's work
Trusted, sharp, first choice for the small stuff.
Just a whisper, in those old woods, then dust, forgotten.
But no more of that.
Found you. A fresh file and care.
You'll see those old woods again.

-Jim Bartlett

Dearest Voice in My Head

Dear God, I pray you—just a voice in my brain;
I'm allowed to leave, but, God, just let me remain.
I need not a life; as the white pillars do sheen,
White pillars I'm not, but what scurries between.
Passing through—this life—no reason, no plan,
Just to love a good woman, and to kill a bad man.
Give me bright smiles, to fly abreast a gnashing of teeth,
Give me bright skies, and I shall stay underneath.
And if such skies can keep forever blue,
I'll know it wasn't in vain, this prayer to you.

-David Rose

Ranks of White

Morning rays, a golden hue, give to your pale visage
Shadows, banished by the day, lurk in angled lines and draws
I lie in peace amidst dew-dropped curves and blades on which you lie
A blanket, born of heavenly breath, warm and safe beneath the sky

An echo, a mourn, not seen but felt, a memory long ago
A flash of light, a flash of sound, age-faded but crisp and bold
Loving assault upon senses, dulled, these memories to the fore
O'ershadow the triumphant trumpets' call to a friend in need no more

Eyes lift from the green to the playful draught, teasing brilliant stripes
with ease
Starry night turns starry day, watched by timeless guardians, freed
A dance in the wind, the fabric plays, with its furl and snap of cloth
Watched over by beams of radiant gold, free of want and grief and wroth

Wondrous gaze falls to alabaster skin, in blessed relief, stark
By warmed touch, your closed eyes have kept me through the dark
A spot of color, here and there, my eye is drawn toward
As light's embrace engulfs the forms lying there upon the sward

In it forms remembered touch, a soft caress of fabric bold
Nevermore to be prepared, to put hot iron to patch and fold
Hang up your cartridge belt, my friend, stow horn and save your shot
I recite familiar phrase, echoed in time, "I have the watch"

A duty ends, a soul at rest, I stand after the night
And turn my gaze to hallowed rows
Of marble ranks of white

-Bryan Moulton

Ghosts of the Khyber

(Originally published in *Ghosts of Babylon*)

Last night I had the strangest vision
As I lay asleep on my cot
I dreamed we were out on a mission
And I must have gotten lost

For I found myself alone on "a darkling plain"
Under a star-filled black green sky
I looked for the rest of my platoon in vain
They had vanished in the night

So I set out resolutely for the horizon line
Across that vast and rocky plain
And after awhile I began to climb
Into the foothills of a mountain range

And as I climbed higher
I felt the air getting lighter
And I climbed ever higher
Into the Khyber
Into the mountains of the Khyber Pass

And as I labored through the darkness
I saw a light gleaming bright through my NODs
I could see it beneath a rocky escarpment
And moving figures, as through a fog

I worked my way closer to this light
And was surprised to find there
A well-established bivouac-site
And in the center, a roaring fire

And there beside the leaping flames
Three figures were reclined
They laughed and joked without restrain
And drank from skins of wine

A more motley group I could not imagine
How they came together baffled me
They wore the trappings of infantrymen
But from different stages in history

The first had a weapon with a familiar profile
I picked him out first from the rest
By his side was a Kalashnikov rifle
And he wore fatigues and a load-bearing vest

The second wore a bright red jacket
And an ammo belt with leather straps
On his head was a white pith helmet
And he sported a striking mustache

The third of the three was the most unique
He had a circular shield and a long spear
He wore only sandals and a red tunic
His face had been worn by the years

And they sat by the fire
And the flames leapt up higher
And they drank by the fire
In the shadow of the Khyber
In the shadow of the Khyber Pass

They saw me standing, a bit removed
And called me over to the fireside
They bade me sit and eat their food
And offered me some wine

"Relax, comrade," said the first of the three
"From us you have nothing to fear
We've all been fighting the same enemy
And we're all on the same side here"

For he had launched raids against the same mujaheddin
As a member of the Soviet Spetsnaz
And did helo-borne raids just like me
And fought in the same valleys and draws

"At last," he said, "it came to an end
When our bird went down in a fiery crash
Just over there, around that bend
In the shadow of the Khyber Pass"

The mustached man had found a bottle of gin
At the bottom of his old rucksack
He flashed at me a knowing grin
As he tilted the bottle back

"It was here I also met my fate,"
He said after he finished his swig
"It was late in the year 1878
At the Battle of Ali Masjid"

"We were shoulder to shoulder, charging en-masse
I remember it vaguely, like a dream
As we stormed their fort at the top of the Pass
And I died a loyal soldier of the Queen"

"A tribesman's arrow was what did it for me,"
Said the third with the weathered face
"When I came through here in the fourth century BC
In the army of Alexander the Great"

We finished off the Macedonian's wine
And the Brit shared the rest of his gin
The Russian produced some vodka by and by
And we all commenced drinking again

And we sat by the fire
And the flames leapt up higher
And we drank by the fire
Me and the ghosts of the Khyber
The ghosts of the Khyber Pass

And we swapped war stories for hours on end
About the engagements, large and small
And we cursed the wretched Afghans
And wished death upon them all

At last the hills began to grow light
The morning chill hung damp in the air
The fire sputtered and clung to life
I could barely see the others there

I slowly got to my feet and stretched
"My friends, I must be getting on
Thank you for this most welcome rest
But I can see it's almost dawn"

The Macedonian looked up at me then
A gentle look on his rough-hewn face
"Just sit yourself down and rest, my son,
You've already become one with this place"

"Be at peace, my son, and don't be afraid
You're one with the thousands who have gone here before
And here with their memories will forever remain
In these hills that are older than war"

And at his words, I looked down at my hands
They were faint in the pale morning light
And I knew that now I would never leave these lands

-Jonathan Baxter

Illustrator: Justin Craine

-Epilogues & Epitaphs-

Ode to the boy in Section 60

Here's to the boy who lies beneath the grass.
The one who said yes to the killing,
The one who was willing.
To him, we raise a glass.

Here's to the boy whose head is marked with stone.
The one who entered the world of violence,
The one now retired to eternal silence.
To him, forever prone.

Here's to the boy who came home humbled.
The one who shouldered every load,
The one who walked the lonely road.
To he, who never stumbled.

Here's to the boy adorned in brass.
The one who was eager to volunteer,
The one who forged the tip of the spear.
To him, beneath the grass.

-Mac Caltrider

True Heroes

A girl is asked to name her hero
Holds up her headphones high
Says her hero is the singer
With glamorous, extravagant life

Houses and cars, without a care
She has nothing to want
She lives her life at breakneck speed
Her walk has earned its jaunt

Eyes travel 'cross the old car seat
To a son with dreams of sports
Asked the same question
Who his hero is, of course

Star player for his favorite team
Outspoken, brash, and bold
His size and strength command the young
To follow in his mold

In silence the journey carries on
Both speakers had their chance
The boy pipes up, in a curious voice
"Who is your hero, gramps?"

A quiet turn of the steering wheel
Down an off-ramp goes the car
The old man searches through the trees
For a quiet place to park

Still silent he leads the children forth
Through sunlit meadows green
A slight mist rolling under foot
Gives the appearance of a dream

In front of a plain steel pole he stops
And drops down to his knees
The flap and furl of hallowed cloth
Can be heard above the trees

Wide eyes search 'round for meaning
In the ranked white stones around
Flowers, flags, and medals
At the base of them abound

"This man saved my life two times"
The children hear him say
"This one shared his meal with me,
They got him the next day"

These men fought beside the others
Without prejudice, hate, or sneer
They answered the call of a nation
Good men, from far and near

Now they protect everyone
Hated, loved it matters not
With brothers, fallen, their post is walked
Their vigil will never stop

For their brothers, left and right
This price they gladly pay
Remember true heroes near and far
On this Memorial Day

-Bryan Moulton

Make Sure it's Warm

When I die,
Bury me at sea; just make sure it's warm.

When my heart no longer spasms,
Release my remains in space,
-The one measured in fathoms
Where the great ships rest among unexplored chasms

Bury me at sea; just make sure it's warm.

My remains to be recycled, do not delay
Don't confine me to cold ground,
Where sole duty is decay
I welcome the silence; I've retired from the fray

Bury me at sea; just make sure it's warm.

Cast my body off in the Carolinas or the Keys
Don't pay any mind if it's the bullet or disease
I'll have a crew in no time,
Old salts home in heavy seas

Don't trap my body in some rural grave
Don't leave it locked in a crypt or a cave
Rotting like a dingy church with a half-hearted congregation,
Visitors coming once a year out of obligation.

Bury me at sea; just make sure it's warm.

I'll be happy down there,
At one with nautical lore.
I'll no longer need my regulator, or fins to explore.

Don't imprison me in cedar,
Nor incinerate me either,
Ya
Bury me at sea;
Just make sure it's warm.

-Mac Caltrider

Of Electricity and Other Mysteries
(Originally published in *Ghosts of Babylon*)

our chemicals
chimerical
comprise our existence
in instants of emissions
electrical transmissions
synaptic firings like fireflies shining
in a fibrous web woven
by midnight spinners
Weird Sisters
glowing and gleaming
sparking and igniting

like scintillations from foundry machinery
or the arc of a welder's torch
or immolations in a porch bug lamp
winged messengers fried at two thousand volts
singing their last note on a millisecond death row
luminous ascensions like a log's leave-takings
flying up a flue
or distant glowings like marsh fires reflecting
in poisonous poolings
or enraged red as angered embers
blown by a bellicose bellows
or other-worldly like electric haloes forming
around rotor blades churning through the sandy night
fire-forged in strife

the roars, the rushes, the loves, the hushes
existent in a self-consuming instant

and the price we pay for these
ephemeral firings
selling your life away in the Middle East
whiling the time away for the pay and the hope
of another endorphin chain-reaction
firing like a 5.56 belt
rushing into a gun's hungry breach
burning, then fading into the sky
like tracer rounds reaching through the night

or lost, looking for the floating and then the drowning
in the flowing from the mouth of a bottle
the bar beckoning with a panoply of glass fingers
the liquid lurking in the low light
gleaming with a silent, heavy expectancy
promising lethe, nepenthe

or in the voodoo rattle of a prescription pill bottle:

promises, promises
pop this, pop this

step right up, step right up
this'll pick you up
yessir, yessir
that's not hissing you hear
no snake oil sold here!
lookee, lookee, nothing up this sleeve
this'll grant you your reprieve

take two with water
costs a dollar
but for you
I'll sell it to ya for four bits
you can't pass up this

I promise this
promise this

we must pick our potions sagely in this
Olde-Thyme Emporium
Whether it's a golly-gee ice cream and sodey-pop float
(cherry on top)
or one of the darker specimens floating
in jars behind the counter
we must craft our concoctions carefully, to be sure
mixing the distilments, elixirs, unctions, and tinctures

designing the lightning we are going to be riding

else we become that pile of rags and smells
holding a sign, "Veteran---Please Help"
or wrapped in a car's broken, metal embrace
and bloody kiss
dreams and promises racing through our veins

promises, promises
I promise this, promise this

trying to describe our lives in the space
between the flash and the thunder's crash

fireflies entangled and consumed
in a web of our own spinning
trapped and blinking
out our last beats

as we bleed out in the wreckage heap
or pass out in soiled bed sheets
or hang our heads alone to weep
or burn in a high-altitude freefall
because Icarus-like we tried to touch the sun
or in a vehicle fire in some foreign place
because, moth-like, we drifted to close to the flame

we must choose our combustions carefully

as our lighting bug lamps
and blazing oil fires
burn out in the night

overhead, the stars are constant in their cold-clear light

-Jonathan Baxter

MDCCLXXV

(a response to Inscriptions for Headstones)

rest in peace man who thirteen days before 9/11 at twenty-five left the civilian world to enlist in the navy because the Marines didn't need as many infantryman yet and so instead became a bodyguard for navy chaplains and served with Marines and discovered that the Marine Corps world had different customs and rules: like speed and violence of action accomplish missions, and sometimes it is appropriate to kill a fly with a sledgehammer, and running far and shooting straight helps kill bad guys before bad guys kill Marines, and in garrison shit bags don't polish boots or starch cammies or get weekly haircuts, and also call people by their rank because there is a chain of command that dare not be broken or tested because in combat it has been tested and will not break, hasn't broken in 239 years, and saying nah or yeah instead of no or yes is a good way to get an ass chewing and so is having your hands in your pockets and while we're at it, stand up straight, shoulders back, chest out, look people in the eye and sound off when you talk unless the enemy is present and clean weapons, then gear, then body is the order in which things are done and packing light means freezing at night but packing heavy means carrying that shit on your back which gets old so learn to pack necessities and be an alpha male and earn the respect of the other alphas and every other word is fuck but sometimes kill or oorah and everyone is warrior or killer and the most dangerous weapon in the world is a Marine with his rifle but more frightening is two bored Marines and fuck those people who say dip and smokes are unhealthy, we run towards gunfire because when that first bullet comes, running towards it saves lives and every Marine is a leader who wants to save lives and if a senior Marine is killed the next senior one takes charge and continues to fuck shit up and the twenty-year-old corporal or twenty-two-year-old sergeant makes the life or death decisions so listen the fuck up when he talks and eventually you call that corporal or sergeant by his name because you are brothers and you will kill the bad guys before they kill your brothers and if you die in a combat zone they box you up and ship you home but it doesn't matter since your brothers will never forget you because you are immortal

-Michael Ramos

-Epilogues & Epitaphs-

Solitude

this life i live is mine to choose, this life i love of solitude
this life i live is mine to rue, this life i live of solitude
this life i live is mine to lose, this life i live of solitude

i wake up each day, tired and hurting
results from many years of working
i awake each morning, my heart a-hurting
a result from wounds still scarring

i sit and watch the clock arms ticking
a dog who tends his wounds by licking
yet those scars i keep picking
to give myself a job, wounds that need licking

-Matt Horning

Soft

Part of me has grown soft, but it's probably a good thing.

Last night I watched half of a turtle try in vain to drag itself off the highway.

A few years ago that would have been endlessly funny.

Now I can't stop thinking about it.

-Mac Caltrider

Strawberry Fields

To the point of no return
A slip away from the cliff
More like a sip away from the drift
A return is all I look for

Clarity and sobriety
Identical twins that look fraternal
Visions brought to light within the nocturnal
The stars and sun become allies

Too much to achieve
A moment changes the course of time
Alcohol dilutes feelings by silencing the mind
Why can't I think straight?

Perception is defined by *blurred* lines

-Tyler James Carroll

Always

Have you ever wanted to live? Like really live?
Have you ever wanted to die? Like really die?
And not really know why…either way
Then one day, BOOM!
Suddenly you realize why you want to live,
But what gives?
I'm up, then I'm down,
Busy silence all around,
Unseen tears falling down, down, down.
The constant pain in my head,
"Turn from the violence," is what they said.
And I did.
No motion, just commotion,
My painted ship on a painted ocean,
Waiting, contemplating,
This resting place ideal,
Still what I feel, is fucking real!
And it's raw, and it's pain,
It's pressure insane,
My brain, my brain, my brain!
But, everybody hurts, like R.E.M.
But my R.E.M. can't even begin
Until whenever these constantly running thoughts get caught somewhere
and come to an end.
And again, and again
I'll never know when
I will, have sweet dreams
Because it constantly seems
That when my eyes close
The blackness exposes
My inability to productively,
Become someone's muse,
While I quietly abuse,
This Zolpidem that I got from him,
Or the Fluoxetine, that's replacing the Sertraline, that was making my
stool turn green…
Causing me to be unseen
From many places,
And the stillness replaces,
The chatter and smiles,

And many, many miles on an empty road,
Is what I desperately need
To help me unload
And show clear.
I don't fear, death,
I love each breath, that I take
So what makes, me
Emotionally unprosperous,
What good is all this phosphorus?
Atomic number 15, if you hear what I mean.
Now rocking and swaying,
I hope what I'm saying
Resonates, because heaven hates
A liar, so I'll speak the words on my mind
Until I find, a place, to see my face…empty
Of all that ails it.

-Emilio Gallegos

On Fear

I don't know a lot,
but I know one thing
for sure,
I'm not afraid of life,
but it damn sure
should be afraid of me

-Marty Skovlund, Jr

Mine to Write

Every day I have to wake up and reinvent my mind
Like spent brass on the tile
Taking the burden of a lost soul and letting it fall to the floor
Because these shoulders are tired and I can't bear the weight anymore

I know it's not my problem
Truth be told
But if you understood these boots I was expected to fill
You would know the pressure I hold

I didn't just carry that casket and that was the end
I have held that weight in my heart again and again
I can't just go peacefully into this night
Have too much tied into this life

My heart has been torn in so many directions
Not sure what the truth is anymore in my reflection
Is it sad when you can't recognize yourself?
Look at your face and all you see is someone else?

I have lived a majority of my day, thinking
"Was I always supposed to end this way?"
"Was I always going to be in this pain?"
"Was I supposed to teeter on the sane and insane?"

Held guilt for so many years
Why was it I had to see his family in tears?
Handing them the gold star with grief
They looked at me like their child's accomplice…soul thief

Now we battle with conflicts of self and where we stand
We are losing ourselves by our own hand
That hand that feeds the magazine
The hand that holds the weapon
Which shoots the enemy
Hands and fingers made to touch and feel
But instead turned on ourselves for our own lives to steal

Stop reaching for that escape
You should be reaching for that open door of community
You should be letting your brothers in
And asking for immunity

You see, every time I see another person who decided to take the wrong door
It's another battle lost in the big picture of war
We fought, but now we continue to fight for life
We fight out of love of each other
For love of ourselves and significant others

I have cried myself to sleep when no one's looking
I am man enough to say I need help, and I am not joking
I lost myself, and everything that was me
So I became alone
Caged in a savage world, I became angry

I have been there, in a hole so dark
No night vision or flash
Could help me find my path
I have burned myself alive, from the inside out
Alcohol, painkillers, numbing self-doubt

I submit the prescriptions I know I don't need
But if the doctor says so, who am I to disbelieve?
It's like I'm two people: Dr. Jekyll and Mr. Hyde
What you see during daylight isn't the man I am at night

Slurs of an alcohol-fueled slumber
I can still feel it creeping in the blink of an eye
When I turn to my friends, I have lost count and lost hope
Funny thing is, they are in the same boat

We say cheers to the fallen, for sacrifices made
We all know the price, we know what's been paid
We are in the same place; we lost a piece of our puzzle
Still trying to find it, forever in struggle

Sometimes I feel I'm pulled in two separate directions
One minute firmly on feet, the next in depression
I am always two steps from destroying the core

I feel some nights, the best part of me was lost in war
Would they be acting the way that I am?
Living with life, so ready to give in?
I can't believe they would take this so lightly
This fight is not over, it's daily and nightly

Being light infantry isn't just an MOS anymore
My first battle is getting my feet on the floor
Quick to the painkillers, just to gather my vision
Will I make it through today? Will I survive this mission?

What made me this way?
What caused this corruption?
I was such a peaceful child growing up
Now I am struggling just to not self-destruct

Don't think I haven't been there before
In the dark and alone, looking for that exit door
I can't tell you why I didn't choose that chance
My destiny simply isn't ready to be done with this dance

But when it's dark as night and I can't see the light
I remember this is my book, and I'll continue to fight
The last chapter in this life, it's mine to write
Sometimes I feel I'm already halfway in the afterlife
So I call on those who have walked the same roads, dealt with the same fight

Those exposed to what most could never understand
The trials of war, the trials of man
We stand together to conquer the fear
To soldier the weather

Can the weather stop a soldier that's come back
From days that were colder than anyone has ever seen?
I had to intervene
Because I awoke from a dream

One of you struggling with the demons of war
I know what you feel, I've been there before
I know you have my back
And I have yours.

-Vincent Vargas

A Room Full of That

I look at him and wish my life was that easy.
He looks at me and wishes his life was that exciting.
I talked to a guy today who felt he never lived an exciting life,
Never really done anything.
But I envied him.
He still had his wife, his kids.
Got to enjoy them every day after leaving his simple job.
I, on the other hand, I have a crazy-exciting job
and I go home alone
and don't get to see my kids every day.
At the end of the day, when I am on my deathbed,
I hope someone will be there to hold my hand as I go.
He will have a room full of that.

-Vincent Vargas

Reflections at Appomattox: The Surrender of the Army of Northern VA

It is but a memory now,
that tiger, living as it did.
Treading the land,
its world moving with it.
Claws, blood, fire,
rain and mud.

A quiet, soldierly salute,
from a foe valiantly fought.

Then gone like a mist,
over a river with the coming
of the morning sun.

Dissolved into the ages,
but never forgotten,
that it passed this way.

-Jim Bartlett

Life of an Exile

America is my land,
Heaven is my home, but
I have lived through Hell.
I want you to know me, yet
I am unwilling to know you
if we can't meet on common ground.
Perhaps, I expect too much
or disclose too little. But,
please tell me why fitting in is so uncomfortable.
It is as if,
I walked a mile in a pair of shoes that have never stepped on anything
that would scuff up something that was designed to work.
But I get it, because
if I roll up my sleeves-
I break dress code, and
being a man
has become a sin against humanity.
That's neither here nor there, but
it is no wonder why
I feel like I
don't belong anywhere.

-Tyler James Carroll

God, bless those heathen boys

God, bless those heathen boys
they who worship you not,
for they are forever my brothers,
and spilled crimson blood is our lot.

Lord, bless those heathen boys,
the best men I'll ever know,
who have fought Them and They
in sea, in sand, in snow.

Father, save those heathen boys,
they who carry the sword.
They give their sweat, their hearts, their lives,
all more than they can afford.

Jesus, take care of those heathen boys
who worship with wine and beer.
They drink to remember song, to laugh,
and to wholly forget their fear.

Creator, bless those heathen boys
who take women for a night of pleasure.
Their time is short and brutal on earth,
filled with pain without measure.

Sovereign, save those heathen boys,
forced to drink the cup of hate and rage,
for they must survive their world of war,
they are fed death, and blood is their wage.

Spirit, watch over those heathen boys,
though they have their vices and sins,
For the best Christians aren't perfect.
We all fight the savage within.

Christ, take in those heathen boys,
for they are without a home.
They return from war changed and scarred,
and in their own nation they restlessly roam.

-Cokie

Memory Lane

Took a stroll down memory lane,
It was littered with IEDs.

Just wanted to think about old friends,
Instead my mind had to sweep every step.

Thought I might reminisce on good times,
But found myself picking up lost limbs in place of lost stories.

Don't think I'll take another stroll for a while,
At least not in search of laughs.

-Mac Caltrider

The Cycle Repeats

I'm doing that thing again.
The vicious cycle of self-loathing and narcissistic ambition.
Stuck in this loop of anxiety and energy.
I look down at my bare wrist where the watch usually sits and realize my
time is fading and its well past time for sleep.
Where do the hours go?
Where did the meaning all go?
My life used to have purpose but now just routine.
Wake up
curse my insomnia
blaspheme the little sleep I managed to bargain from the tormentors in
my dreams.
Shower.
Dress.
Coffee.
Work.
Misanthropic nihilism.
Dinner.
Dwell.
Nightmare.
Repeat.
This cyclical journey of purposeless wealth acquisition only to divvy out
my earnings to pay for things I don't have the time to enjoy.
The adventures of my youth now turn to a peppering of gray in my hair
and beard. Growing older and losing perspective of the dreams I once
chased with reckless abandon.
Where did all that faith go?
How has my hope died?
Why did the man behind the curtain at Oz have to be a fraud?
Can someone please pull the wool over my sheepish sleep deprived
sunken eyes? I would rather be blissfully unaware than educated in the
deceptions of church and state.
It's time for sleep.
Those nocturnal demons of wide eyed stimuli perpetuating this vigilant
awareness of my finite existence.
Close my eyes.
Bid my time.
Maybe tomorrow will be that elusive "One Day" that everything
changes.

-Stan Lake

White Noise

There is such a rage inside of me. I do not understand it.
It washes over me and I lose myself in its noise.
I always wake up to the feeling of your warm tears on my skin and the
smell of smoke from the bridges I burnt.

-Nicholas Rossin

Suicide Poem

Shooting myself would be easy. I know it would hurt, and I know it's
selfish.
That doesn't change the fact that I don't want to die yet. At the same
time, I died a long time ago.
So what's the harm
in suck starting a forty-five, when everything around you seems
pointless?
We lose people every day, And every day we mourn, So why not have
people mourn me?
It's the will to live and push through the bullshit and bring yourself to the
side of happiness.
This side is the light side, full of joy, charisma, and elation. Real
euphoria.
Full of family, friends, companions, lovers, and life. The kind of
happiness that pushes you
To continue living on this beautiful planet,
The kind of paradise that brightens the darkest days. The kind of
perfection you realize is there halfway into writing your suicide poem.
The light is there. Everyone is there. We are here.

-Justin Eggen

The Winter Man

I once met a man
On a last winter's night

He had leathered skin
And one eye that pierced like a January gale
His heart was cold
It had long since frozen over

He contained a quiet rage
But deep down
I knew there was nothing quiet about it
He hadn't been given a fair shake
Not in this life at least

He told me, "you gotta live hard"
As the wind whipped around him
Circumstance brought us together
But why without shelter?

"Do you have a place to go?"
I asked, as snow drove into my face
He replied, "We all do, I hope"

I didn't expect such optimistic words from a man
that society had long since forgot about

He wasn't a bum, he told me, appearances aside
A traveling man, he replied, when I inquired about his occupation
The wind and the snow and the teenage temperature
Didn't seem to disturb this stoic of the road

I couldn't understand him well, but I'm not sure that was his aim
I felt sorry for him, but he knew that look all too well
"My pa and the war did me wrong," he replied to my gaze
"But the road never has, not once."

"It's a cruel bitch, but a fair one," he went on
"Driving snow, falling rain, hot sun, or scorching asphalt…
The road treats you the same as it treats me."
It was at that time that my Uber arrived
I felt ashamed to get in, given the circumstances
But the look from his one eye, and the smirk on his face
Told me he felt sorrier for me, than I did for him.

-Marty Skovlund, Jr

Bleed on the day, bleed on the night
Bleed on believing that things are alright
Bleed on the one who stayed by your side
Bleed on their family, along for the ride

Shoulder the task, do so with pride
Shoulder the guilt since the day they died
Shoulder the tears their widows cried
Shoulder the stone, shoulder the spine

Break the back, break the bone
Break the water that molds the stone
Break the guilt and come back home
Now break the cycle of bleeding alone.

-Leo Jenkins

3495 Bailey Avenue

Every step, a set of ribbons stitched on a hat
Reminding you of where they've been and where you're at
Wedged in a chair, relating more to the peeling linoleum
Narcotics more present than the fiends who are holding them
We are the resolve and we are the end result
We are the hammers, the scalpels and the old salts
We are more though and moreover
We are walking, talking textbooks when the war's over
As rattled as we wanna be
As broken as we all believe
When they read our story, what will they take away?
Will they know of the triumphs or will they pity our decay?

-Keith Dow

Living on the Wind

I bled my life as to live on the wind,
Pondering if old scars would float their own way.
If the wind should carry; lock, stock, and barrel,
The panoply of pain; shared in dismay.

The thing with blood is — upon it so frowned,
Seen violently spewing, then a heart rests still,
But it's what made that same heart, hard, once pound!
Allowing for passion, and folly, and for thrill.

Bled my very life, and there it did pool,
With dead roaches and a once-bummed smoke,
With gym bags and war flags; oh, how a king did rule,
A laugh for despair, and some tears for a joke.

But the jokes no more, levity be gone,
Wished I'd laughed more when they were still there,
But now just over, what made the king or the pawn,
So I bled my life as to fly on the air.

Bloodless I flew, yet the jokes were still loud,
The jolly mirth did bellow, far and wide,
The boastful man; still he simmered so proud,
But nobody gawked when he turned, hid, and cried.

So I flew back down, to my little red sea,
Back to a bloody mess and its momentous strife,
I tried to suck it all down, back inside me,
But someone was busy now— taking my life.

Alright, I should just admit my act,
I screamed then chased that blood-sucker for a day.
For it was my life, my blood, my puzzling contract,
To read, breach, cherish, or plain throw away.

You feel me on this, when your trash gets picked?
Ya' feel violated—this villain straight out the movies,
Thorough, thieving hands; ya' got plain simple nicked,
And suddenly what ya' tossed; its diamonds and rubies.

-Epilogues & Epitaphs-

Well, came back, this blood-sucker, he sure did,
My eyes fooled, I thought, for sure, from blood loss,
Met with a great big handshake, this damn kid,
Said "I too gave my life the big hefty toss."

"Then why in the world take mine?" I exclaimed,
"What a trade," I said, "old trash for new garbage.
"Youngster, you'll be better off, wild and maimed,
"Then gulp up all my deeds and that carnage."

This little shit, though, at *wild* that smile broke to roam,
And my trash trickled as his thoughts unfurled,
"I always," he said, "felt; the stranger at home,
"But at home in the wilds of the world."

We flew then together, he took me to his own pool,
Dribbled out, and right then being sucked clean,
By someone else, some god-awful fool,
Who'd felt the world had treated another flyer less mean.

Pool after pool, bless me, pile after pile,
Those who felt Life a thief 'sted a giver,
Dotted lesser pains, than his or I, for a mile,
And lesser pain's blood became a red raging river.

And now, when some sorry voice cries a sad plea,
Its miseries; born upon it too young,
I carry them, as that boy had once done for me,
By pain alone; do we see heaven's gifts hung.

I say, "See this open, endless sky, so pearly,
"Below us, through pain, begat your brother and friend.
'We paid life's quota of pain so damn very early,
"And now free to live on the wind."

-David Rose

More than Our War

I still remember when, we stood together then, boys becoming men, seeds becoming trees, becoming corpses, walking. I still remember the day we learned to hold our own amid the smell of innocence, burning. I still remember when.

The ones returned still burned, this time from the inside. Night after sleepless night, begging to feel less alive. The ones returned unknowingly earned, the underserved honor and burden born of medals worn and countless brothers now to mourn; the weight of each a stone, to fill the pack upon our back, until the load snaps bone, testing our apt to atone.

Now, to pull the stone from the pack upon our back and save the snap of bone. I learned we are worse alone. Came together once more, brothers reborn. And with that stubborn stone, built a towering thrown where now we sit and see through burden bore, a forever endeavor to be, but let us be now,

More than our war.

-Leo Jenkins

-AUTHOR BIOS-

Joe Barnhill served in the U.S. Army from 2010 to 2018 as a platoon leader with the 73rd Engineer Company, 1/25 Stryker Brigade Combat Team in OEF. He achieved the rank of captain.

Jim Bartlett served in the U.S. Army from the late '80s to the early '90s as a combat engineer before he ETS'd and joined up with the Croatians as a volunteer. He later became a war photographer and disaster responder.

Jonathan Baxter served in the U.S. Army from 2005 to 2011 in 3rd Battalion, 75th Ranger Regiment, achieving the rank of sergeant. In 2016, he published a poetry anthology titled *The Ghosts of Babylon*.

Daniel Lee Brown served in the U.S. Marine Corps from 2004 to 2015 as a member of 1st Marine Raider Battalion. He is the producer and host of The Dangerzone podcast and a creative artist who goes by the name "Daniel The Barbarian."

Dwight Buchanan served in the U.S. Army in 2012 as an infantryman in Aco 2-121 48th IBCT, then as a member of scout platoon from 2014 to 2018. He currently serves in the National Guard serving on the military funeral honors detail and has attended more than 500 funerals for veterans and active service members.

Mac Caltrider served in the U.S. Marine Corps from 2009 to 2014 as a rifleman with 2nd Battalion, 8th Marines. He is currently working toward completing his first book.

Tyler James Carroll was a Combat Medic for 173rd Airborne Brigade. After his service he and his wife returned to Texas, and he became a firefighter and father. Tyler co-founded Dead Reckoning Collective and co-authored *Fact & Memory* with his old Army buddy, Keith Dow.

Cokie served eight years as a U.S. Marine Corps scout sniper in Iraq and Afghanistan. He did some time as a PMC, then joined the National Guard as a medic, where he is still a sergeant. Cokie has previously contributed writing to OAF Nation.

Bryan Crosson was commissioned as a Marine Corps officer after graduating from The Citadel in 2010, then went on to serve as an advisor to the Afghan National Security Forces. Bryan has previously been published by the Veterans Writing Project and is currently pursuing a Masters of Business Administration from Georgetown University.

Keith Dow is a born New Englander, who has been writing ever since he could hold a pen. He spent 5 years on active duty in the US Army before being honorably discharged in 2013 to start a family. Keith co-founded Dead Reckoning Collective and co-authored *Fact & Memory* with his old Army buddy, Tyler Carroll. At this point, Keith is best known for being the only US Army veteran living in Canada with A-M-E-R-I-C-A-N tattooed across his knuckles.

Justin Eggen served in the U.S. Marine Corps from May 2008 to 2012 as a combat engineer with the 2nd Marine Division. He's published three volumes of poetry: *Outside The Wire: a U.S. Marine's Collection of Combat Poems & Short Stories Volume I, Volume 2*, and *The Art Of Warrior Poetry*. Additionally, Eggen has a signature clothing collection.

Charles Faint is a career Army officer. He holds five undergraduate and graduate degrees, the most recent of which is from Yale University. He served seven tours of duty in Afghanistan and Iraq and over the course of his career was assigned to units including the 101st Airborne Division, the 2nd Infantry Division, the 5th Special Forces Group, the 160th Special Operations Aviation Regiment, and the Joint Special Operations Command. He also served as an instructor at the United States Military Academy at West Point for five years, and was the head of West Point's "Officership" capstone program for two of those years. Widely published in a number of blogs and professional journals, he is a Fellow with West Point's Modern War Institute, and is co-authorship of the book *Violence of Action: The Untold Stories of the 75th Ranger Regiment in the War on Terror*.

Emilio Gallegos served in the U.S. Marine Corps during Operation Iraqi Freedom, where he received a Purple Heart after receiving wounds from an IED in 2008. He found his love again for the arts through writing therapy at the Palo Alto VA, Polytrauma Rehabilitation Center. He has been a participant in the San Jose Poetry Festival in 2016 and 2017, and has been a featured reader on YouTube's Central Coast Poetry Show.

Kellen Gumm served in the U.S. Marines as a hospital corpsman second class during Operation Iraqi Freedom and Operation Enduring Freedom, then as OEF 3rd Btn 1st Marines Wpns Co-OEF 1st MarDiv RCSW police training team.

Laura Hamlet served in the U.S. Navy from 2012 to 2015. Hamlet is a writer, actor, and director.

Clay Hildreth served in the 3rd Ranger Battalion from 2008 to 2011. He has found writing to be an excellent exercise in his transition to civilian life.

Matt Horning served in the U.S Army as an infantryman for nearly six years and now works as an EMT while going to paramedic school.

Leo Jenkins served three combat deployments as an Army Ranger medic with 3rd Ranger Battalion from 2003 to 2006. He is the best-selling author of several books including *Lest We Forget*, and *First Train Out of Denver*. Leo currently resides in southern Baja Mexico where he spends his time writing, painting, and raising his daughter, Kezia.

Ryan Kisner currently serves in the U.S. Navy, stationed on the USS Hopper DDG 70, and has been active duty since 2015. He's served two deployments to the 5th and 7th fleet AOR. Ryan is currently working on a soon-to-be-released novel.

Michael Krukowski served in the U.S. Marine Corps as a sergeant for 10 years, deploying three times to Iraq. He's currently a stay-at-home dad to two kids and a baby who just went through two major heart surgeries. He's been writing since he was 13.

Stan Lake served in the North Carolina Army National Guard, enlisting a week before 9/11. He served in the 5-113 Field Artillery as a MLRS crewmember before the unit was repurposed to do convoy operations in Iraq/Kuwait in 2005-2006, during which time he became a .50-caliber gunner on a Humvee gun truck. He's published three children's books and a nature/faith book, as well as a documentary about his former unit in Iraq titled *Hammer Down*.

Curt Last served in the United States Naval Reserves as a hospital corpsman from 2008 to 2016, during which time he served in various Navy hospitals and deployed to the Role 3 Combat Hospital in Kandahar, Afghanistan. He has a master of fine arts degree in poetry from California State University, Long Beach.

Robin Ludwig served as a Health Services Manager in the 136th Medical Group (USAF ANG) since 2002 and has volunteered for multiple humanitarian and hurricane response missions. She has taught literature and writing in Texas and England, and is the author of *Help! A Monster Ate My Brain* and the co-author of *Behind the Ranks Vol. 3.*

Moises Machuca served in the Marine Corps from 2007 to 2017, leaving as a sergeant. He was with 2/7, 3/5, and finally with the Marine Corps Mounted Color Guard.

Neil MacKinnon served seven years in a British light infantry regiment.

Paul Martinez is a veteran of Operation Enduring Freedom, retired Ranger sniper, freelance print journalist, and author of his memoir, *When the Killer Man Comes.*

Barrett McCulloch served in the U.S. Air Force from 2009 to 2017 in the 720th Special Tactics Group, achieving the rank of staff sergeant.

Marshall McGurk served nearly 5 years with the 3rd Special Forces Group (Airborne) after a stint with the 4th Infantry Division (Mechanized). He enjoys scotch, cigars, good books, foreign films, and critical thinking. He is passionate about international relations, domestic affairs, and successful veteran transition.

Nick Misiano, aka Charlie Moose, served four years in the Marine Corps Infantry from 2001 to 2005, deploying throughout the Pacific Rim and Iraq and fighting in the Second Battle of Fallujah. He left the Marines as a corporal. Charlie wrote and self-published a book titled *Lava Dawgs* based on his experiences in Fallujah.

Bryan Moulton served 12 years in the United States Marine Corps. He was medically separated and is currently attending veterinary school.

Jonathan O'Brien served as an 0311 with Golf Company 2/8. He deployed to Ramadi, Iraq in 2007 and Helmand Province, Afghanistan in Summer 2009. After the Marine Corps O'Brien graduated with a bachelor's degree from Clemson University and is now a Center Lead at the NASA DEVELOP Program at Langley Research Center. Jonathan O'Brien runs the Combat Art Collective.

Michael Ramos served in the U.S. Navy as a Greenside Religious Program Specialist in 1st CEB and 2/4, First Marine Division during the invasion of Iraq. He holds a bachelor's and master's of fine arts from UNC Wilmington, where he teaches creative writing. Michael is a contributor to OAF Nation Hitter Feed. His essays have appeared in The Sun and Fourth Genre.

Branden Ray served in the U.S. Army's 2nd Ranger Battalion from 2008 to 2011.

David Rose served in the United States Marine Corps from 2002 until 2006 as a member of 2nd Recon Battalion. He is the acclaimed author of *No Joy* and *From Sand and Time*.

Zack Shier served as an Army Ranger in the 1st Ranger Battalion from 2008 to 2012.

Marty Skovlund Jr. served as an Army Ranger in 1st Ranger Battalion from - to -. He is the best-selling author of *Violence of Action: The Untold Stories of the 75th Ranger Regiment in the War on Terror*. Skovlund continues his pursuit of storytelling as a journalist, photographer, and filmmaker. He is currently the executive editor for Coffee, or Die Magazine.

Christian Sonnier served as an Army Ranger in the 3rd Ranger Battalion.

Vincent Vargas served as an Army Ranger in the 2nd Ranger Battalion. Since his time in service, Vargas has appeared in several movies, authored his own memoir, *Light the Fuse*, and most recently held a main cast role in the hit television show, Mayans MC.

-ACKNOWLEDGMENTS-

Thank you to Nate Granzow at Venator Media solutions for his diligent editing services.

-REQUIRED READING FOR THE CONTEMPORARY POET WARRIOR-

From Sand and Time: Poems
Winner of the Robert A. Gannon Award.
The first official poetry installment in David Rose's unique blend of tenderness and morbidity, From Sand and Time engages a cataclysmic self-reflection coming with the complexities, times, and demands of the wars in Iraq and Afghanistan. An evocative collection of rhyme and free verse, From Sand and Time weaves through ambition and belief, doubt and loneliness, deployment, combat, and what waits thereafter.

With a Pen
A raw, evocative, and intelligent collection of poetry from best-selling author, Leo Jenkins. Jenkins utilizes a lyrical style to express observations about truth, love, war, and the world around us.

Outside the Wire: A U.S. Marine's Collection of Combat Poems & Short Stories
A soul-searing collection of poems and stories from the front lines of Helmand Province, Afghanistan. Author Justin T. Eggen experienced two combat deployments in Afghanistan, Marjah 2010 & Sangin Valley 2011, fighting the Taliban (and occasionally the weather) with his brother warriors. Back from the front, he wrote this masterful description of the realities of war. Many of the poems are haiku, a form at which he shows great adeptness. Mixed in with the poems are three slice-of-life stories dealing with the everyday life of Marines in combat.

The Art of Warrior Poetry
The third instalment from Justin Eggen. A poetry collection that explores the psyche of the writer going from adolescence to war, to returning to society a broken soul.

Fact & Memory
A collection of poems from the founders of Dead Reckoning Collective, Keith Dow and Tyler Carroll. Fact & Memory is about growing up, trauma, loss, love and happiness. Mostly it is about getting a lot of things wrong before you start getting them right and how you remember those events versus how they actually happened.

The Ghosts of Babylon
Eyewitness accounts of warriors who lost their innocence dueling in the sands of the Iraqi inferno or fighting in the chilling Afghan mountains or on the khaki-colored plains. Wounds enshrouded under the bandages of headlines and sound bites will never bridge the gap between soldier and civilian.

Only a soldier poet lays bare the honor and horror. Only a veteran reveals the physical and mental battles waged by the warrior caste. Only the war poet distills the emotions of those who tasted bravery and terror, love and vengeance, life and death. Based on the experiences of a U.S. Army Ranger turned private security contractor, these powerful poems capture the essence of Jonathan Baxter's twelve military and civilian deployments.

Jonathan reveals the contradictory nature of deployment in a war zone—exhilaration, monotony, ugliness, and occasional beauty. From ancient times to present day, war poetry telegraphs a dispatch across the ages about the universal experiences of war—brotherhood and bereavement, duty and disillusionment, and heroism and horror. No history mirrors the brutal realities and emotions of armed conflict than the shock of war erupting from the warrior poet's pen.

Jonathan resurrects the ghosts and gods of soldiers past. His poignant memorial to fallen brothers transmits the shadowy presence and ultimate sacrifices of the coffined to the fortunate un-coffined. The Ghosts of Babylon strips away the cultural varnish of the 'enemy,' painting the bitter irony of everyday lives caught in the crosshairs of terror, chaos, and death. From moving to startling to soulful, these masterpieces provoke you to think about the truths and consequences of those who risk their lives on the frontline of freedom—for you, their friends, and our country.

The Shape of Our Faces No Longer Matters
Poems by decorated Iraqi Freedom veteran Gerardo "Tony" Mena, the first book in a new military-service series. The Military-Service Literature Series is a continuance of the collaboration between Missouri Humanities Council, Southeast Missouri State University Press, and Warriors Arts Alliance that produced the anthologies Proud to Be: Writing by American Warriors Volumes 1 and 2. The poet, Gerardo Mena, is a decorated Iraqi Freedom veteran. He spent six years in Special Operations with the Reconnaissance Marines. He was awarded a Navy Achievement Medal with a V for Valor for multiple acts of bravery while under fire. His work has been published in such journals as Baltimore

Review, Ninth Letter, Prairie Schooner Online, Cream City Review, Poetry East, Cider Press Review, and War, Literature and the Arts, among others. His awards include the 2010 War Poetry award, Missouri Humanities Council's National Veterans Poetry Competition, the 2011 Penumbra Haiku Contest, and inclusion in Meridian's Best New Poets 2011 anthology.

-FORTHCOMING-

Lava Dawgs: A Fight for Fallujah
Charlie Moose

An infantry battalion of Marines from Hawaii, find themselves deployed to fight in the biggest, urban battle since the Vietnam War. The city of Fallujah, in al-Anbar Province, Iraq, has been hijacked by a foreign, Islamic fundamentalist insurgency, that is hell bent on attacking Americans and torturing and killing Iraqi civilians. The Marines are tasked with ridding the city of the jihadist fighters and giving it back to its people. Lava Dawgs is a down and dirty perspective of grunts on the front lines of urban combat.

Discrimination of War
Tyler James Carroll

A Combat Medic from the 173rd Airborne Brigade connects the various walks of life that the men in his platoon lived prior to enlisting in the military. The men in his platoon were pressed to identify and relate differences in order to create a unified organism. His platoon endured the death of one of its own, and Carroll shares the struggles and triumphs those men experienced leading up to that moment and the lasting effects War had on them. If War was personified it would be indiscriminate to its participants, and Carroll believes War can teach man how to truly love.

Revolutionary Veteran Support Network®

GallantFew's mission is to prevent veteran isolation by connecting new veterans with hometown veteran mentors, thereby facilitating a peaceful, successful transition from military service to a civilian life filled with hope and purpose.

We do this by creating and supporting a nationwide network of successfully transitioned veterans that engage locally with new veterans with the same military background now going through transition and by motivating communities all over the nation to take responsibility for veterans returning; welcoming, connecting, and including.

CONTACT:

Karl Monger, Executive Director
Mobile: 817-600-0517

info@gallantfew.org

gallantfew.org

gallantfew

gallantfew

WAR POET SOCIETY

The War Poet Society is the rally point for battlefield poets. This anthology was the organization's brain child. WPS is also known for initiating the Verses & Curses Tour, an open mic series encouraging poet warriors to share their experiences via spoken word, music, poetry, and more.

The War Poet Society will be taking future submissions for *In Love... &War: The Anthology of Poet Warriors Vol. II* beginning April 2019.

versescurses@gmail.com

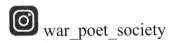 war_poet_society

Made in the USA
Columbia, SC
21 March 2019